FIRST IN THIRST

First in Thirst

How Gatorade Turned the Science of Sweat Into a Cultural Phenomenon

DARREN ROVELL

AMACOM AMERICAN MANAGEMENT ASSOCIATION
NEW YORK ▸ ATLANTA ▸ BRUSSELS ▸ CHICAGO ▸ MEXICO CITY
SAN FRANCISCO ▸ SHANGHAI ▸ TOKYO ▸ TORONTO ▸ WASHINGTON, D.C.

Special discounts on bulk quantities of AMACOM books are available to corporations, professional associations, and other organizations. For details, contact Special Sales Department, AMACOM, a division of American Management Association, 1601 Broadway, New York, NY 10019.
Tel.: 212-903-8316. Fax: 212-903-8083.
Web site: www. amacombooks.org

This publication is designed to provide accurate and authoritative information in regard to the subject matter covered. It is sold with the understanding that the publisher is not engaged in rendering legal, accounting, or other professional service. If legal advice or other expert assistance is required, the services of a competent professional person should be sought.

Library of Congress Cataloging-in-Publication Data

Rovell, Darren, 1978-
  First in thirst : how Gatorade turned the science of sweat into a cultural phenomenon / Darren Rovell.
       p. cm.
Includes bibliographical references and index.
  ISBN 0-8144-7299-0
  1. Gatorade (Firm) 2. Beverage industry—United States. I. Title.

HD9348.U54G38 2005
381'.4564126—dc22

                                                                    2005013242

Printing number
10 9 8 7 6 5 4 3 2

CONTENTS

ACKNOWLEDGMENTS IX

INTRODUCTION 1

CHAPTER 1: SWEAT IN A BOTTLE. 9

The Guinea Pigs and Testing 15

Making the Drink 17

The First Test. 19

The LSU Game 21

CHAPTER 2: THE MYSTIQUE IS BORN 25

The Auburn Game. 29

Gatorade Snatchers 30

Press Catches On. 33

Commercial Interest 38

CHAPTER 3: FROM FIELD TO SHELVES **41**

In Gatorade They Trust 44

Marketing Issues 46

NFL Coolers and Cups 50

Sports Illustrated 53

Cyclamate Disaster 58

Continuing the Legend 62

CHAPTER 4: WRESTLING OVER GATORADE **65**

The University Loses Out 68

The Trust Takes It to Court 71

Cade Explodes 72

It's All Settled 74

CHAPTER 5: THE "TIPPING" POINT **77**

The Inaugural Dunk 78

Carson and Parcells Get Paid 80

Best Gatorade Baths 86

The Deadly Dunk 88

CHAPTER 6: "BE LIKE MIKE" **95**

The Thirst Aid Campaign 97

Wooing Michael Jordan 99

Jordan Signs $13.5 Million Deal 102

"Be Like Mike" 105

His Airness Retires 115

CHAPTER 7: "WE'RE GOING TO WAR" **123**

Coke and Pepsi Attack 124

All Sport Dismantled 131

1996 Olympics 138

Convenience Store Strategy 139

POWERade Relaunch 145

NASCAR Battleground 150

CHAPTER 8: THE GATORADE RULES **153**

1. Make Sure Your Product, Service, or Brand
   Is Unique and Know What Makes It Unique 154

2. Never Stop Researching the Marketplace 158

3. Identify Drivers of the Business and
   Take Care of Them 163

4. Never Stop Working to Get Your Next Consumer 168

5. Packaging Counts 172

6. Learn from Your Mistakes 175

7. Seek to Connect Emotion and Passion to the Brand 178

8. Stay Disciplined 182

9. Form Smart Strategic Alliances 188

CHAPTER 9: GATORADE CRITICS **191**

Quaker Buys TQ2 193

Pedialyte and Rehydralyte Challenge 196

New Challenger 199

Gatorade vs. Water. 200

Influence Over Trainers 203

The Dehydration Myth 206

EPILOGUE. **211**

APPENDIX A **215**

Sponsorships 215

Origins Ad. 221

Everywhere Rap 223

Gatorade Royalties. 224

Gatorade Sales 224

All-Time Flavor Roster 226

APPENDIX B **227**

Letter Exchange, Bill Schmidt and Bill Parcells 229

NOTES **231**

INDEX **239**

ABOUT THE AUTHOR **244**

ACKNOWLEDGMENTS

This was a book I had to write, but I couldn't have done it without the help of so many people.

To my family—Mom, Dad, and Brian—who didn't hesitate when, less than a year after my first book was published, I started on this one.

To Ruth Gordon, Mark Gordon, and Abbey Rovell, thanks for being such a good, loving support system.

To Michael Pokrassa, a great friend who went with me on runs to Holiday Farms to buy our first Gatorades.

To Jenn Scherz, for the love in your heart and always having a Gatorade in your fridge for me.

Thanks go to those at ESPN.com—Kevin Ball, Wayne Drehs, Tom Farrey, Andy Katz, John Marvel, and Marc Stein. Each of you has taught me something about how to be a reporter. And to my bosses, Neal Scarbrough, John Papanek, and John Kosner, for allowing me to pursue this project.

To my Gatorade angels—people who helped me carry the story—Ed Ansel, Dana Shires, and Bill Schmidt, thanks for putting up for my incessant e-mails and always being available.

To Bill Ferrara and Evan Appell, please don't tell anyone how little I paid you. You guys volunteered hours and hours of your time, and you never disappointed me. I hope this book gets you a foot in the door somewhere.

To the folks at Gatorade, who were supportive of this project from the beginning. Thanks go to Andy Horrow, for having faith in me; to Heather Mitchell, who worked countless hours to set up interviews and compile important data; and to Karen Hunter, who despite her everyday workload found time to read this book twice for accuracy.

To Bonnie Block and Adam Tanielian at Fleishman-Hillard, thanks for letting me talk Gatorade with you. And, of course, to all the former employees who worked on the Gatorade brand over the years, thanks for helping me preserve your history.

My extreme gratitude goes to Gary Klotz, Matt Troyer, and Kelly Eskew at Bingham McHale for introducing me to the Gatorade Trust and telling its members about the importance of telling their story.

To Steve Orlando, Kay Howell, Steve McLain, Patrick Reakes, and Barbara Wingo at the University of Florida and to Dan Habing at the U.S. District Court in Indianapolis. I couldn't have done all this research without your having everything ready when I stopped by. And to Kerry Tharp at the University of South Carolina for helping me track down Steve Spurrier at the last minute.

I appreciate the proofreading done by my colleagues, particularly David Carter, Asher Golden, and Ben Sturner. To my agents at RLR, Jen Unter and Tara Mark, thanks for continuing to fight hard for me.

And finally to the folks at AMACOM, including Christina Parisi and Jim Bessent, who believed in my vision and helped me get this incredible story out to the world.

FIRST IN THIRST

AS A SEVENTH GRADER on the Roslyn Middle School cross-country team, I wasn't exactly an asset. Thanks to my occasional walking during races, I finished so far behind the pack that my scores were almost never counted in the team standings. Some people might have given up, but there remained one thing that validated my worth as an athlete. Luckily, 16 ounces of the magic potion could be purchased for $1.29.

Others might have bought Gatorade as the juice that gave them that extra edge, but for me, it wasn't about staying hydrated. I couldn't have cared less about the science behind it all. It wasn't about the great taste, either. I mean, who really wants salt in their drink?

It was not as clear then as it is now, but holding that glass bottle in my hand and drinking the very same yellow, red, and orange concoction that was guzzled by all the athletes I admired made me feel as if we had a bond.

Wheaties could call itself "The Breakfast of Champions," but I never really believed it. Did you ever see the athletes featured on the box chowing down on those flakes? There definitely weren't spoons and bowls scattered on the playing field.

I was sure that Gatorade was the "Drink of Champions." Every place I watched, either in person or on television, there were those big orange coolers full of it. Pitchers who had just struck out the side would go into the dugout, grab a green waxed paper cup with the Gatorade logo on it, and refill themselves with the special substance that would certainly give them another inning of success.

For as long as I could remember, NFL players would hoist the Gatorade cooler and dump it on their coach, surely a sign of homage to the drink as much as it was to the coach himself, at least to this 14-year-old.

So while others in my grade worshipped Right Said Fred for his rendition of "I'm Too Sexy," the official theme song among my clique was "Be Like Mike," the Gatorade jingle featuring Chicago Bulls superstar Michael Jordan, which was introduced less than a year before my graduation.

Before I knew anything about sports marketing, I thought that every team had Gatorade on the sidelines or on the bench because if they didn't, they were pretty much forfeiting the game. I knew it wasn't in the official rules, but I thought that every team just understood that Gatorade was the 10th batter in Major League Baseball, the 12th man on an NFL offense, and the 13th man on an NBA bench.

As I grew older and learned more about the business, I started to understand that the omnipresence of the brand was part of a well-targeted strategy. Gatorade had amassed a network of thousands of sponsorship deals worth hundreds of millions of dollars (at least $135 million was spent on advertising alone in both 2003 and 2004[1]) that required leagues and events to give the brand a significant presence.

Today, more than 60 Division I-A schools are under contract to use the brand, as are 28 of the 30 NBA teams. Gatorade is guaranteed to be the official drink on the sidelines of every NFL team through the 2011 season, thanks to a deal that was signed in February 2004 that pledges that the brand will pay the league more than $45 million per year. The brand is also a large part of the amateur sports scene, sponsoring thousands of road races and active sporting events as well as awards for high school athletes in all 50 states and the District of Columbia.

It's one thing to have a great marketing plan. It's another to execute it to near perfection, as those who worked on Gatorade's brand have done over the years.

That being said, all the marketing in the world won't create sales if the product isn't any good. I might not have cared how or if it worked, and I'm sure scores of others didn't either, but it must have helped.

Only once did I associate Gatorade with failure—when Chicago Cubs second baseman Ryne Sandberg accidentally spilled a bucket of the drink on first baseman Leon Durham's glove 10 minutes before the start of the fifth and final game of the 1984 National League Playoffs. Durham's error in the seventh inning of the game helped the Padres take the lead and eventually win.

"The glove got heavy and sticky after the Gatorade spilled on it," Durham said.[2]

But for every Durham error, there were scores of stories that associated Gatorade with a winner—real stories about real athletes who supposedly gained a real advantage from sucking it down.

Like the story of a harness horse named Manfred Hanover, who in 1985 won an astounding 24 of 46 races. In 1986, the horse was recognized by *Sports Illustrated* after prevailing in 16 straight races. The secret for the horse, whose father was aptly named Super Bowl? Drinking 200 gallons of orange Gatorade each year.

In 2004, 19-year-old Olympic swimmer Michael Phelps tied Mark Spitz's American record by winning eight medals at the Summer Games in Athens. When he bought his mother, Debbie, a new Mercedes, he told her it was "for all the Gatorade you bought me."[3]

The Gatorade mystique doesn't involve just those in the sports world. Its legend has been affirmed in the most untraditional of environments, most recently in the story of five-year-old Ruby Bustamante. In April 2004, a guardrail repairman in California found Ruby and her mother in a ravine 130 feet below the highway after a car accident that had occurred 10 days before. Ruby's mother had died immediately as a result of the crash, but Ruby survived, thanks to somehow having the wherewithal to ration the uncooked ramen noodles and Gatorade that happened to have been in the car. Gatorade and Nissin Foods, the maker of the noodles, reportedly donated $5,000 each to establish Ruby's college fund.

Gatorade has become one of the most perfect products in American consumer history. The drink itself has meaning, an unshakable marketing platform, and a sales force that has refused to give up anything to its competition. This has led to an 80 percent market share throughout the better part of the drink's existence.

The *New York Times* named Gatorade one of the 100 best brands of the 20th century—along with the beverage kings Coca-Cola, Pepsi, and Budweiser. But consider that Pepsi and Coca-Cola's share of the U.S. soft drink market combined does not equal Gatorade's share of the sports drink market. Anheuser Busch, maker of Budweiser, had its best year ever in the United States in 2003, with its domestic market share topping out at 49.8 percent—paltry compared to Gatorade's 80 percent.[4]

Sales of shoes for Nike and Reebok combined don't equal the market share that is enjoyed by Gatorade. Only a select few companies can claim such a high market share, such as Intel (about 80 percent of the U.S. PC processor market), Apple (about 80 percent of the U.S. digital music player market), and eBay (about 80 percent of the online auction economy).

Although I felt like drinking Gatorade made me part of a unique club, I obviously was not alone. The drink is a favorite of former vice president Al Gore, it's the frequent liquid of choice of *Hustler* publisher Larry Flynt, and fictitious sports agent Jerry Maguire pulls orange Gatorade from the fridge in his office in the movie of the same name. Even two of the most popular bulls on the Professional Bull Riders tour, Little Yellow Jacket and Slim Shady, have Gatorade in their water troughs before they go out each night.

It has a loyal following in the music world, too. Elvis chugged Gatorade during his comeback tour in the early 1970s, and the sports drink soon became the required dressing room beverage of R.E.M., KISS, Luther Vandross, and Tom Petty. The members of the group The Moody Blues led all musicians in quantity—requiring 27 liters of lemon-lime Gatorade for every show.[5]

As players on the football team at the University of Florida drink it, so too do the Gators fans, who on average, consume 10,000 Gatorades while sitting in the stands during home games.[6]

Just as it is as relevant to athletes and fans alike, it also has its uses in less traditional environments. Gatorade has saved the lives of children in third-world countries suffering from diarrhea, and its concentrated powder has been a relief to American soldiers fighting abroad who are sick of the taste of water or need more salt in their diet. It has been offered as a homemade remedy for the common cold and menstrual cramps and can also be used as a toilet bowl cleaner and as bait for roach traps (along with sliced raw potatoes).

Gatorade plays an integral part in alcoholic drinks, such as the Anti-Freeze (Gatorade and vodka) and Green Crap (green Gatorade and gin), and is also used to prevent hangovers the next morning.

When I graduated from Roslyn Middle School, Gatorade came in only a few sizes and a handful of flavors, and the drink grossed about $800 million in sales for its parent company, Quaker Oats. Thirteen years later, there are more than 30 flavors in eight different bottles on the market worldwide, and the brand is sold in over 50 countries, with gross retail revenues surpassing $3 billion in the United States alone.

Over the past 40 years, more than a hundred sports drinks that hoped to compete with Gatorade have come and gone. Within the past 15 years, Gatorade has held off Coca-Cola's POWERade and Pepsi's All Sport. It has driven brands like Nautilus, Powerburst, Enduro, BodyAde, Dragonade, Starter Fluid, and Quenchade into extinction, in part because its own Gatorade Sports Science Institute has funded more than 100 studies that demonstrate the efficacy of its product and, sometimes, the lack of worth of its opponents.

It has not won the battle by engaging in price wars or changing the formula of the drink. Gatorade has prevailed because the product works and because those commanding its brand, for the most part, have stayed focused on the sports drinking occasion. These brand managers have developed innovative ways to break through the clutter—from tangible brand identification through its coolers to behind-the-scenes hard work with trainers and convenience store managers.

That's one of the reasons why Gatorade is virtually everywhere. It can be found every day in gas station store refrigerators in Seattle, Washington, on pretzel carts in New York City, and on supermarket shelves in Key West, Florida. Squeeze bottles filled with it can be seen in the hands of NFL players playing on well-groomed fields in front of more than 60,000 people and in the hands of young boys playing a pickup game on the rough concrete courts of Detroit, Michigan, in front of a crowd of six onlookers.

In 2000, Sue Wellington, then president of Quaker Oats's U.S. Beverage Division, said, "When we're done, tap water will be relegated to showers and washing dishes."[7]

She wasn't kidding. Today, more than 100 billion ounces of Gatorade are sold in the United States each year, which means that approximately 12.2 million bottles of Gatorade, or 142 bottles per second, are sold in America every day.[8]

But despite this dominance, the in-depth story of how the 40-year-old brand was conceived as a lab experiment and went from being an undesirable drink to an icon recognized throughout the world is relatively unknown.

In 2002, Gatorade commissioned a survey to discover just how many people knew about the drink's origin. Results revealed that 60 percent of the people polled didn't know that the concoction was invented at the University of Florida for its sports team, the Gators. In fact, 26 percent thought that the drink's name came from a fictitious inventor, "Dr. Lawrence Gator," and 2.1 percent thought the name came from the drink's secret ingredient—alligator juice. When given a range of choices, only 11.2 percent of those polled knew that the brand was nearly four decades old.[9]

This is a classic business story. It begins with four doctors—one of whom had recently come from Cuba with $5 in his pocket. They devise a sports drink formula as a side project, with the idea of solving a scientific riddle rather than making a mint.

Through a series of fortunate transactions, their invention finds its way into the hands of some very shrewd businesspeople, who craft a relevant strategy, learn to evolve over time, and stay one step ahead of those who are striving to grab a piece of the pie.

In the process, the story winds up mimicking the world of professional sports that Gatorade ultimately helped serve. This tale is one of teamwork and timing, but it is also wrapped in fortune and greed.

* * *

This account is based on the recollections of the people involved. In an effort to come up with the most accurate portrayal of events, individual memories, which are subjective, sometimes had to be reconciled. I believe that the vast number of people interviewed, combined with my judgment, has yielded the most truthful account possible regarding the elements of the Gatorade story written about in this book.

CHAPTER 1

Sweat in a Bottle

IN THE BASEMENT of the pharmacy wing of J. Hillis Miller Health Center, in a room with unfinished floors and protruding pipes, surrounded by piles and piles of canned foods saved for a possible atomic attack, an eccentric nephrologist and his colleagues were working at a feverish pace.

Most university labs are closed at 8:30 p.m., but these fluorescent lights were used to putting in overtime. Dr. Robert Cade, a 37-year-old associate professor of medicine who specialized in kidney disease, and his research fellows at the University of Florida were carrying out yet another experiment. And, since they knew that the next day their magic potion would face what was sure to be its largest test yet, there was no time to spare.

It had been a month since Dewayne Douglas, a former University of Florida player who was an assistant coach of the university's freshman football squad, had sat down to lunch with Dana Shires, one of Cade's fellows whom Douglas had befriended in his other role as the hospital's chief of security.

On that day in August 1965, Douglas, who had been named to the All-Southeastern Conference (SEC) third team as a senior in 1952, told Shires that the freshman team was in bad shape. Over the weekend, 25 players had been admitted to the hospital's infirmary because of heat exhaustion and dehydration.

This was a serious matter. In the 1960s, as many as 25 football players across the country died each year from heat-related diseases. In Florida, some of the players were losing more than 15 pounds during every game. Seeking a solution, Douglas (who said that he had lost as much as 18 pounds on some game days) pleaded with Shires to come up with something to negate the strain that the brutal summer heat had inflicted upon his players.

Players who drank too much water would get stomach cramps, while players who put too much salt in their bodies would often experience leg cramps. After Shires filled Cade in on the conversation, the two wasted little time.

Making the perfect drink for football players wasn't exactly a priority. Cade, who had joined the University of Florida's medical department in 1961, was working on slightly more heady research projects, such as the regulation of sodium levels in rats.

He had classes to teach and patients to worry about. At the time, the University of Florida was one of only a few places in the country where doctors were performing kidney dialysis. But given Cade's history of mixing drinks at his hepatorenal (liver-kidney) symposiums, there was no chance that he would pass up the idea of making a concoction in the best interest of science.

Every Friday, the lab was the most popular place to be in the hospital, as the 5-foot-7 Cade gave a quick 20-minute lesson and then prepared various drinks in beakers and test tubes for the audience. It was no wonder that he was named the most popular teacher in the medical school for two straight years.

It wasn't so much that Cade thought that some day one of his ideas would make him millions. He was far from being materialistic. Take, for instance, the fact that, despite making millions over the nearly 40 years that Gatorade has been on the market, Cade and his wife, Mary, still live in the modest ranch house that they had called home before the product was even invented.

For Cade, it was more about using science to solve problems. He was particularly intrigued by the fact that football players rarely had to go to the bathroom during a game, or, in Cade's words, "to wee."

It didn't hurt that Cade was also a big sports fan. He was so enamored with the St. Louis Cardinals that after graduating from Southwestern Medical School in 1954, he saw to it that his first internship was at the St. Louis City Hospital, 630 miles away. That was a short distance from Sportsman's Park, where he could see Red Schoendienst and Stan Musial hit and Harvey Haddix pitch.

Cade was beginning to fall in love with the Gators, and he and the others knew that replacing fluids would be a true advantage for the team, as the athletes' loss of fluids led to dehydration, serious salt depletion, and in some cases severe heat stroke. Luckily, Cade—himself a former high school track athlete—had a group of eager young medical school fellows who, despite the strain of their daily work, were willing to follow their leader. Shires, in particular, also had a fascination with sports. He had played high school football in Florida.

Cade and Shires were aware that a decent amount of information about the physiology of body temperature was available. Sweat was made up of more than water and salt, but they weren't quite sure of its exact composition.

Cade sent one of his other fellows, Alex DeQuesada (a Cuban who had arrived at the university just one month before), to the library to learn about the formulation of sweat. In just two hours, DeQuesada returned with almost everything that had ever been written about the topic.

In addition to DeQuesada's research, Cade and Shires were armed with a paper they had received at the 57th annual meeting of the American Society for Clinical Investigation, which had taken place in Atlantic City just months before. At the meeting, Dr. Sidney Malawer, who had been a medical resident at the University of Florida the year before, had presented his findings on how water, salts, and sugars are most effectively absorbed in the body.

Malawer concluded from his studies that a beverage containing salt and glucose (a sugar that didn't need to be broken down) would move into the body much more quickly than water in one section of the small intestine. A curious Shires and Cade (surely not knowing how they would ever apply this interesting information) took Malawer out for a lobster dinner the night of his presentation, asking questions and absorbing his study.

The conversation turned out to be important for the doctors months later, since they wanted to invent a drink that would be immediately beneficial to athletes as they were playing the game. Malawer had done his experiment on 18 men, but the University of Florida doctors needed to study athletes in order to figure out the amount of salts they needed to replenish.

So Cade and Shires went to the office of the team's head trainer, Jim Cunningham. There, they told Cunningham, Douglas, and the University of Florida's varsity head football coach, Ray Graves, that they would need to use the players to determine the proper amounts of ingredients for their solution.

At most college programs at the time, even water wasn't readily available. One school of thought was that dehydration would toughen up players. The on-the-field success of torture artists like Paul "Bear" Bryant, who didn't let his players rehydrate themselves in any fashion, didn't help change things. Bryant won 323 games at Maryland, Kentucky, Texas A&M, and Alabama. But the doctors explained to Graves that the machismo attitude that had been pervasive in sports was actually hurting the performance of teams run by stringent coaches.

While some coaches adhered to the extreme philosophy practiced by Bryant, other coaches were more lenient. Some allowed their players to practice sip-and-spit—at games and practices, the players would swish water around their mouths before spitting it out. Others provided a cold, wet towel that the team would bite on, trying to strain every last drop of water out of it.

More-progressive coaches provided players with salt pills to replace the sodium lost when players perspired. Unbeknownst to many coaches and trainers at the time, however, the salt pills had the potential to raise the sodium in the body to harmful levels.

Graves knew plenty about the tough-coach philosophy. He didn't practice it, but he had had to endure it as the star center of three University of Tennessee squads that went 28–4 throughout his career. Even as captain of the 1941 team, his legendary Tennessee coach, General Robert Reese Neyland, provided players like Graves only with a lemon to suck on during games and practices.

The doctors told Graves that if they were able to devise a solution that would replenish what the players lost through sweat, it would prevent the players from becoming dehydrated and could even help make them stronger than their opponents in the fourth quarter of games.

Graves didn't exactly understand the biochemistry and physiology behind the reasoning, but he agreed to do it.

"Coach Graves deserved a lot of credit for sticking his neck out and trusting the doctors," said linebacker Chip Hinton, who played on the freshman team, the "Baby Gators," in 1965. "He realized the bottom line was to win, and if it could help us, he was all for it."

Graves didn't give the doctors a carte blanche. After being assured that the fluids would be safe, he worried that they would affect performance. He didn't want his elite athletes serving as any kind of guinea pig.

"You can take the freshmen and do anything you want with them," Graves said. "But you can't mess with the varsity team." Sometime later in the conversation, Graves added Larry Rentz to the "do not touch" list. That meant that Rentz could drink the solution, but he could not be tested and prodded by the scientists.

Rentz was a highly touted quarterback from Coral Gables Senior High School who had never lost a game throughout his entire high school career. He was well-known in Florida because his team had won the state championship in his junior and senior years and because the championship game in his senior year, against Tampa Robinson, was televised for the first time. He was so coveted that coaches from Florida, Miami, and Georgia Tech had called his mother at home and at work incessantly until the day he finally settled on heading to Gainesville to play for the Gators.

Graves's concern was understandable. Even though he was convinced that the potion was safe (the doctors had assured him that there would be nothing toxic in the solution), no one knew what it would do in terms of performance. The freshmen were his future, but he was starting to turn the University of Florida into a school with a serious football program, and he didn't need to have any of his best recruits, who were now upperclassmen, negatively influenced by some experiment.

Since taking over in 1960, his team had averaged more than six wins per season, and Florida's only wins against teams that finished the season in the top 10—Penn State (1962), Alabama (1963), and LSU (1964)—had come under Graves.

In fact, Florida's 10–6 victory over quarterback Joe Namath and No. 3 Alabama in 1963 was the Crimson Tide's first loss in Tuscaloosa in more than five seasons of Bear Bryant's leadership. After that loss, the team didn't lose again at home until 1982.

The Guinea Pigs and Testing

With Graves's approval, Cade, Shires, DeQuesada, and another fellow named Jim Free soon began attending practice for the freshmen. Prior to 1973, under NCAA regulations, freshmen were not allowed to play varsity.

On each day of practice for one week, they brought a temporary lab to the field and used two freshmen per day for their subjects.

"We were using humans for our scientific experiments," said Free, who as a research fellow was working with Cade on renovascular hypertension. "In today's world, we probably never would have gotten away with that."

But at the time, doing something like this was not considered unethical. The participation was up to the players, and they were never told that they had to participate.

The first day, two of the freshmen team's largest players, 6-foot-2, 242-pound tackle George Dean and 6-foot-6, 244-pound tight end

Jim Yarbrough, served as the lab subjects. They were picked in part because their veins were so large, making the blood tests easier. The doctors collected preworkout blood and urine samples, and the players put on special rubber gloves that ran up their arms, to collect all the sweat. Finally, the players were injected with Evan's Blue Dye to measure the blood volume.

Throughout the two-hour practice, Dean and Yarbrough dumped the sweat collected in their gloves into a bucket. And when the practice was over, the doctors took additional blood and urine samples. They then brought the samples back to the lab to analyze the numbers. Both Dean and Yarbrough, on this scorching hot day, had lost about 25 percent of their total body sodium, an amount that could have been lethally dangerous.

"We did it in part because we thought what they were doing could change the sport," said Dean, whose arm turned black and blue after one of the doctors missed one of his veins taking a sample that day.

If the players ever thought the doctors were going too far, they told them so. One thing that Dean and Yarbrough did not agree to was having their "true" body temperature tested. Cade and his fellows readied the rectal thermometers, but the two players (and the other eight that followed them) thought that that was a little bit much.

Since Dean and Yarbrough, and the eight other players who were studied later in the week, missed their postpractice training table meal, the reward came courtesy of Dr. Cade. After the tests were finished, the two players (along with Shires) packed into Cade's 1964 Studebaker station wagon for the three-minute drive to 1900 S.W. 13th Street. Attached to the Holiday Inn there was one of the best restaurants in Gainesville, General Gaines Steak Room & Lounge.

"This is not a ringing endorsement of General Gaines," Cade said. "There were only six restaurants in Gainesville at the time, and four of them were hamburger places." NCAA regulations made it clear that Cade couldn't pay the players $5 each, but at the time, he was allowed to pay them by paying for their steak—or make that two steaks. Dean and Yarbrough, as well as most of the other subjects, were so hungry that they ordered the Chateaubriand for two for themselves.

It was expensive for Cade. He spent $111 on dinners in one week, and his university salary for the 1965–66 school year—as an assistant professor and the head of the division of renal medicine—was $16,000.

But at least Cade would eventually have something to show for his investment. With their research in hand, it was now time for the doctors to make the drink.

Making the Drink

The simple idea of the sports drink was to replace fluids lost through perspiration. Sweating occurs when the amount of heat produced during exercise surpasses the amount of heat released by the body. In order to regulate temperature, water from the bloodstream and the cells is evaporated into the air through sweat.

Sweat is mostly made up of water and various salts (or electrolytes)—sodium, potassium, and magnesium—which are essential to the electrical and chemical balance of the body and aid muscle and nerve function.

Since the body, on average, is about 65 percent water, fluid lost needs to be replaced. Dehydration can cause headaches, dizziness, and muscle cramps, with heat stroke being the most extreme result.

The doctors had to concoct a solution—water enhanced with sodium and potassium—that would move through the body quickly to maintain fluid and salt balance during workouts. The doctors then added a mildly sweet simple sugar (glucose) to immediately raise the players' blood sugar and provide them with that extra energy boost.

Their science made sense. Forty years before Malawer's findings, medical researchers had found a link between sugar and athletic performance for athletes who exercised for a long period of time.

Since concocting this drink wasn't part of their daily business, they used the late afternoon for coming up with the most effective potion. Mixing of the solution began immediately. The original solution was colorless and didn't taste particularly good. Cade immediately vomited it out, while others in the lab took small sips around the sink, holding down most of what they ingested.

"We knew that the players weren't going to be all that fond of the taste," recalled Shires, who noted that the first drink tasted much like toilet bowl cleaner. "But we didn't know a damn thing about flavoring."

At this point, the doctors weren't thinking about whether the solution would one day reach stores. All they knew was that it tasted so bad that the players would probably never drink enough of it to make the difference the doctors had hoped to make. They needed to make it tolerable.

After going to the Thirsty Gator, a popular watering hole in Gainesville, Cade returned to the lab the next day with 60 lemons to put into the drink. The four doctors squeezed 20 of them before the drink's putrid taste was finally masked. Batches of the product were inconsistent from day to day, and the early reviews, at least for the taste, were not too positive.

The First Test

The drink's first real test—for both taste and effectiveness—came on October 1, 1965. The "Baby Gators" played four games against conference opponents in their season, and on one of their off weeks, they played the traditional matchup against the varsity B team in what was dubbed "The Toilet Bowl." Even though the freshmen usually had more raw talent, the B team was always favored thanks to having more experience and size. This day was no different.

The freshmen had Rentz and his roommate, a gifted running back from Tampa named Larry Smith, who had actually played against Rentz in the state championship in 1963. Smith went on to play with the Los Angeles Rams and Washington Redskins after his All-American career at Florida. But, by most accounts, the B team's offensive and defensive line had about a 20-pound body mass advantage, which was usually the "X factor" in determining the game's outcome.

With Coach Douglas roaming the sidelines coaching the freshmen and Coach Graves checking up on the performance of his varsity second stringers from the press box, the first half went as expected: The B-team players, who came out of the locker room with toilet paper taped to their helmets, jumped to a 13–0 lead. But the second half was owned by the freshmen. They scored touchdown after touchdown and didn't give up a point the rest of the way. The youngsters easily edged the veterans. Maybe the raw talent was too good, but perhaps it was also the difference in sideline beverage. The Dixie cups on the freshman sideline were filled with Gatorade, while the B team was drinking water.

The doctors never did poke needles into Rentz, although his performance while using the drink that day eventually gave Graves more confidence in it.

Dr. Robert Cade with Chip Hinton, a freshman football player with the Gators in 1965. (University of Florida Sports Information Department)

"Gatorade definitely helped," Rentz said. "I remember feeling the lift it gave me after I drank it."

The freshmen apparently didn't tire out like the B team did, which was one of the original purposes of the drink, as Cade and Shires explained to Graves in his office during their first meeting.

"There was no place hotter than Florida Field," Smith said. "And in those days, drinking wasn't part of the routine, so we were happy just to have something. I was losing a lot of weight from sweating, so I was glad we had it."

Smith didn't need to lose any weight. He was 6-foot-4 and 200 pounds, and he had to wear specially made pants with elastic to keep them from falling from his small hips.

Though the concoction seemed to help, Graves was still hesitant and was not convinced that it worked. But after this last game,

Cunningham was convinced and ordered a batch of Gatorade for the varsity team, unbeknownst to Coach Graves.

"Cunningham said that if we asked Coach Graves to use it on the varsity team, he would still say no," Shires recalled. "But Cunningham thought that if it worked, we would be fine, and that's exactly what happened."

This was a big break for the doctors—their drink had survived its initial test and would live for another day.

The LSU Game

The very next day, the Gators were set to take on the heavily favored No. 5–ranked LSU Tigers in Gainesville. Almost all of the Tigers' key players from their Sugar Bowl championship team the previous year had returned, and in the first two games of the season they had outscored their opponents 52–14.

But making Gatorade for the entire varsity team was no small task, and that's why the doctors were in the lab late at night attempting to round up enough bottles of glucose to make a 100-liter batch. Cade and his fellows mixed the solution in buckets and poured it into two 50-liter vats that were used for storing distilled water. They put the vats in Cade's son Stephen's little red wagon and brought them to the walk-in freezer on the fifth floor.

The testing environment the next day was perfect—the temperature in Gainesville was hovering around 100 degrees. But since Graves didn't know that there would be Gatorade on the sidelines, the players didn't know that it would be there, either.

"The first time, it just kind of showed up on the sidelines," said Doug Splane, a 6-foot-5, 227-pound defensive tackle who played on the Gators' varsity team from 1965 to 1967.

Behind a table with hundreds of Dixie cups on it were the doctors, who handed the cups of their special juice to the players. Before the players ingested it, the doctors made sure to tell them exactly what they were drinking. The players weren't required to drink it, and that day many didn't.

Cade believed that his product would help the players, although the only evidence he had at this point was the freshmen's performance against the B team the day before. He told them, "This is a glucose and electrolyte mixture. If you drink it during the game, you'll be stronger and feel better in the third and fourth quarters."

The first varsity player to try it was tackle James "Breadtruck" Benson, the heaviest player on the team at 6-foot-3 and 250 pounds. Benson was handed the cup and drank the formula with no problem. Then came Larry Gagner, Benson's fellow offensive lineman, who would go on to play for the Pittsburgh Steelers and Kansas City Chiefs.

"This stuff tastes like piss," Gagner said, pouring the rest of it over his head. All-American defensive back Bruce Bennett came next. He took a swig with little puckering and held it down.

"We used to say that the first samples were so awful it could choke a maggot," said backup quarterback Harmon Wages, who played from 1965 to 1967.

The Gators won that day 14–7, holding off the Tigers. Said Free: "If we had lost, you probably never would have heard of Gatorade again."[1]

The doctors were happy that perhaps they had had a hand in the victory, although that would be a stretch, since not many players partook of the drink during its surprise introduction on the sidelines that day.

After the game, Graves, hearing that the solution had been on the sidelines, ordered it for his varsity team for the rest of the season.

From that point on, Gatorade was not only at games, but also on the sidelines at practice.

Like Graves, all the players needed was a little scientific reasoning to convince them that this could benefit them. The doctors told the players that the advantage of Gatorade over water was that it traveled through the stomach fast enough that they could drink more of it and wouldn't get bloated. Absorption of the solution took place when it was emptied from the stomach into the small intestine.

After the LSU game, the Gators won their next two games, beating Ole Miss and North Carolina State. And it wasn't until the week of the Auburn game that the 4–1 Gators finally knew what to call what they were drinking.

DeQuesada originally dubbed it Cade's Cola. "But that was just for fun," DeQuesada said. "It wasn't carbonated, so it wasn't cola."

Cade's Ade also emerged as a potential name. A host of other ideas were thrown out, but Gatorade—suggested by Jim Free—was the one that stuck.

"It was the lemonade that the Gators drank, so I said, 'How about Gatorade?'" Free said.

"Gator-Aid" was also brought up, but the doctors realized that they probably shouldn't use the "Aid" suffix, since that would mean that if the drink were ever marketed, they would have to prove that it had a clear medicinal use and perform clinical tests on thousands of people.

Within days of the final decision, Free hung a sign on the lab door:

Dr. Cade's Lab
Home of GATORADE
Handmade by Licensed Physicians

CHAPTER 2

The Mystique Is Born

THE GATORS finished the 1965 season a respectable 7–4. But Gatorade wasn't getting any national attention. It seemed as if Cade and the other doctors were still indifferent to making their product succeed in the general marketplace. There was no plan for Gatorade to become the beverage of choice for every athlete, young and old.

But things changed in 1966, when Cade started to become interested in Gatorade as a revenue generator for the first time.

The University of Florida athletic department had paid the doctors $1,800 for the 500 gallons that the football team used during the 1965 season. The price covered the costs, but it certainly did not compensate the doctors for their time. At this point, Cade started to think that his invention might have commercial value and that the team should pay a premium, as consumers did for every product bought in the everyday marketplace.

So, at the start of the next season, he told Graves that the drink would cost $5 per gallon ($1.40 more) to make, a price that Graves said was too high. The coach later backtracked when, on two days in August, 24 varsity players were hospitalized with dehydration and heatstroke. The cost of nursing the players was more than the cost of buying Gatorade for the football team for the entire season, according to Cade.

"That second day, Coach Graves called my house and told my wife that he needed Gatorade at whatever cost for both games and practice," Cade said. "So I told him he could have it—at $10 a gallon."

Cade was suddenly both a scientist and a businessman, but he took it one step further. He went to the director of sponsored research at the university and asked if the university wanted to buy Gatorade, or at least give him $10,000 to keep it afloat. For a cash infusion like that, he was willing to split his profits equally with the university. But the head of sponsored research, Vincent Learned, said that the university wouldn't support that decision.

Cade said that he was surprised, as he believed that they could at least cover their costs by selling to football and basketball teams in the Southeastern Conference (SEC) and the Atlantic Coast Conference (ACC).

"He told me that the university didn't have money to put into something like Gatorade," Cade said. "Since only two out of 20 inventions made it, he was concerned that he would get fired if it didn't work. But he told us that if we wanted to go ahead and make it ourselves, that would be fine."

So Cade did exactly that. He said he went to the bank to borrow $500, which would pay for the making of several hundred gallons.

The Gatorade business was starting up at the perfect time. The performance of the 1966 team gave the doctors a chance to make their drink a nationally recognized icon.

The 1966 Florida Gators team was arguably the best team in the school's 61-year history of fielding a football team. At the time, Florida was by no means a dominant team in the SEC. But Graves, who was also the athletics director, quickly became the most successful coach in the school's history.

Florida also proved to be a better team in the second half, something that Cade and Shires had told Graves that Gatorade would eventually help his team become.

It helped, of course, that the team was led by quarterback Steve Orr Spurrier, who went on to win the Heisman Trophy that year. Spurrier was regularly referred to by his initials, S.O.S, because he often performed so much better in the second half of games and, in the process, led so many come-from-behind victories.

Whether it was the talent of Spurrier and the team or the help of Gatorade, no one will ever know. But Gatorade would soon be credited with, at the very least, helping the Gators' cause.

Spurrier, who broke every school record for passing in a game (289 yards), a season (2,012 yards), and a career (4,848 yards) and total offense (5,290 yards), was supported by senior center Bill Carr, who earned All-American honors with Spurrier that year. Larry Smith, a 19-year-old sophomore, had 742 yards on the ground in 1966, a statistic that gave him the SEC rushing title and earned him SEC Sophomore of the Year.

"I think Gatorade gave us a physiological and psychological edge, and then Steve just made things happen," Carr said. "He had such a great ability to manage the clock that he had us all believing every time we stepped out there."

And it helped that most of the media had picked the Gators to finish 6–4 at best, not the 8–2 record the team did compile in 1966.

When the Gators completed their great season, one reporter suggested at the time that the initial success of Gatorade should have an asterisk next to it, so that all who marveled at the story years later would note that the team actually was extraordinarily talented.

"I don't have any answer for whether the Gatorade helped us be a better second-half team or not," Spurrier said. "We drank it, but whether it helped us in the second half, who knows?"

Had the Gators not been successful, marketing Gatorade might have been a struggle. Just ask Dr. Gerard Balakian, an internist from Englewood, New Jersey, who started giving his sports drink to the Rutgers football team in 1965. Balakian surely wouldn't have wanted to link the team's performance to his drink, Sportade. In its first three years using his product, the team had a record of 12–15. Balakian sold his drink to Becton Dickinson. The drink was acquired many times by many companies over the next three decades, but the concoction never had a chance against Gatorade.

Sportade was an effective fluid replacement drink with slightly less sodium than Gatorade. But it simply didn't have the story attached to it—players weren't going to the hospital in New Jersey at the same rate that they were going to the hospital in Florida, and the Rutgers football team certainly couldn't compete with the nationally ranked Gators as a de facto product endorser. Being tied to a winning program at least made it easier to claim that the drink was working.

"By 1966, everyone on our team was drinking Gatorade," Wages said. "And as long as we were, many of us felt like we could run all day."

"Maybe the credit that was eventually given to Gatorade was deserved," said Norm Carlson, Florida's longtime sports information director, who was actually given a sample of the drink before the "Baby Gators" used it for the first time. "The whole team seemed to get stronger as the game went on, and that was in this terrible heat."

The Auburn Game

Thanks to Spurrier's arm, and perhaps Gatorade, the Gators won their first seven games. The most dramatic victory was victory number seven. The Gators came into the game ranked No. 7 in the country and were 16-point favorites against the 3–3 Auburn Tigers. Florida Field had been expanded by 10,000 seats before the season, and the largest crowd ever—60,511 fans, some of whom had paid scalpers as much as $30 per ticket—was on hand to watch Spurrier engineer another come-from-behind victory.

Down 17–13 at the half, Spurrier and the Gators managed to put up a fight, and the score was tied at 27 with time running out. Spurrier put the Gators in field goal range, facing a fourth and 13 at the Auburn 24. That's when Spurrier himself booted a 40-yard field goal that easily cleared the uprights, and the Gators prevailed 30–27. The kick undoubtedly helped Spurrier beat out Purdue's Bob Griese for the Heisman Trophy. Heisman ballots had been mailed out to voters the week before the game and were supposed to be mailed back by the next week.

By this point in the season, most of the opposition had heard about the new drink the Gators were ingesting during games. If they looked closely at the sidelines, they could see it. In 1965, the Gatorade was on the sideline in huge vats. In 1966, the solution was handed out to the players in milk cartons, supplied by the university's dairy sciences department. This provided the players with a colder drink, as the cardboard containers were frozen before they were brought out onto the field. The colder the drink was, the doctors determined, the more likely the players were to consume more of it. The vats of Gatorade also presented a problem in that the ice would melt and the formula would be diluted.

Something that opposing teams couldn't see was another slight tweak in the formula. Making such a large volume had taken a toll on the scientists. Frustrated with what they called "lemon squeezer's cramp," Cade and his fellows wised up in the second season and purchased lemon extract at $1 a gallon from a company in Frostproof, Florida, about 120 miles south of Gainesville.

Gatorade was now a staple for the Florida Gators, and although the team had begun the season 7–0, Cade wanted to test how much Gatorade meant to the team.

Gatorade Snatchers

On November 5, the Gators were scheduled to play the 6–1 Georgia Bulldogs, in another edition of their famous matchup called "The World's Largest Outdoor Cocktail Party"—one of the longest rivalries in college football. The game has been played in Jacksonville, Florida, since 1933. The location is 73 miles from Gainesville and 342 miles from Athens, Georgia, so it has been considered neutral territory.

There had been many good games between the two, but this was the biggest. At stake was the SEC championship and a chance at playing in any of the major bowl games. Accordingly, a record crowd of 62,800 fans jammed into the Gator Bowl.

The Gators jumped out to a 10–3 lead at the half. But in the second half, the Florida offense didn't score a point, while the defense gave up 23 points to Vince Dooley's talented Bulldogs squad. One of the reasons the Gators might have lost? They were without their magic potion.

According to Cade's unpublished autobiography, Gatorade—in a new flavor, grape—was packed in milk cartons, put on the back of a pickup truck, and driven to Jacksonville by the student trainers the night before the game. About halfway through the trip, two big trucks forced the Gatorade truck off the road. The men in the trucks got out and started dumping the cartons on the ground and stomping on them. The thugs—who Cade says were Georgia fans—then drove off, and the trainers continued on to Jacksonville with only a few cartons left.

The loss turned into a big break for the doctors. If it was hard to prove how much of a force Gatorade was in determining the success of the talented team, here was the proof. Fans of the Bulldogs, knowing that ridding the Gators of Gatorade was their only chance, destroyed the Gators' advantage. Sure enough, they didn't have their Gatorade for the first time that year, and they lost.

"And up until then we'd been a second-half team," Graves said. "Getting better as others wore down. Of course, I wouldn't say not having the stuff to drink was the whole story. That Georgia team had something to say about it, too."[1]

If the story about the Gatorade sabotage seems like a perfect marketing coup, it was. If the tale seems too good to be true, well, it was that as well.

The night before the game, the truck was actually driven by a student athletic trainer to the house of the head trainer, Jim Cunningham. The plan was to leave the Gatorade in the coolers in the truck and drive it to Jacksonville early on game-day morning. When Cunningham and the student trainer went to leave in the morning, they found the milk cartons that had held the Gatorade on the ground.

"I do not know what happened to the Gatorade," Shires said. "But many years later, Bob confessed to me that he was the one who had destroyed the product."

It was undoubtedly as ingenious a concoction as Gatorade itself was, although unfortunately Cade couldn't keep the story straight over time. A few months after the event, Cade told one writer that the Gatorade and the truck were stolen. Four years later, the Georgia Gatorade snatchers story was recanted to Furman Bisher, a writer for the *Atlanta Journal*, who noted that the Gatorade was stolen from the cooler at the university's field house.

No matter what the tale, the result was undeniable: The Gators didn't have the drink, and they lost.

"With its perfect record on the block and its greatest campaign of all time in sight, tragedy befell the Gatoradeless young men,"[2] Bisher wrote.

The week after the Georgia game, with Gatorade back on the sidelines, the Gators pulled another great second-half performance in the hot Gainesville heat. Tied 10–10 at the half against a surprisingly good Tulane team that had gone to an impressive 5–2–1 after playing Miami to a 10–10 tie the week before, the Gators scored three touchdowns in the second half and the defense shut out the Green Wave.

"We definitely felt less fatigued," said Doug Splane, who had a particular dislike for the new grape flavor. "You could tell that they were having a hard time keeping up with us."

The Gators did lose to the Miami Hurricanes the following week in Gainesville, 21–16. Despite the loss, Gatorade still took center stage.

Press Catches On

Up until this point, no one in the media had credited Gatorade with helping out the Gators. But following the Miami game, *Miami Herald* reporter Neil Amdur noticed milk cartons scattered all over the Gators' sidelines. "Are you giving your players milk?" Amdur asked Graves, who was so close to some of the University of Florida beat writers that he would frequently have the journalists and their wives over to his house. "No. We've been fooling around with this stuff for a while now," Graves replied. He referred Amdur to Cade. That same night, Amdur called Cade, who explained how well the experiment was working.

After hearing the tale about Gatorade, Amdur knew that the story would get attention. The writers covering the University of Florida football team at the time often had a healthy competition as to who could turn out the most original copy. They could all easily keep track, since all the local headlines about the team would be printed in the *Gainesville Sun*.

Before filing the story, Amdur called the editors at the *Miami Herald*. "We have an unusual story," Amdur said. "This is pretty unbelievable."

Knowing that the next day's paper would be filled with coverage of the game, Amdur saved his column to run in the middle of the week, so that it would get the attention it deserved.

On November 30, 1966, the story appeared in the sports section.

"A liquid solution that tastes like a mint and works like a miracle may be one of the factors behind the success of the University of Florida football team this year," Amdur began his *Miami Herald* piece, which had the headline "Florida's Pause That Refreshes: 'Nip of Gatorade.'"[3]

Although Amdur noted that nearby Starke [Bradford] High School, which also used Gatorade, finished 9–0–1 and was playing in the state playoffs, Cade had to come up with an explanation as to why the 1965 University of Florida team went 7–4 when it used Gatorade.

"This year is a different solution," Cade told Amdur. "It's been modified . . . we've added a couple other electrolytes." In reality, the formula hadn't been tinkered with at all. Perhaps Cade thought he had to make sure that people thought that it was a newer formula that was doing the trick.

The Gatorade story was picked up by other news outlets, and the story took on a life of its own. But it still wasn't clear that Gatorade could ever be effectively marketed. After all, the reviews in the articles that followed Amdur's weren't all that flattering.

"It's not a good-tasting thing," quipped the sports information director, Norm Carlson. "It's rather bitter. It looks like weak lemonade. It tastes like lemonade too, but not as good."[4]

Cade had done as much as he could to try to tell the story of the drink, but investors and beverage companies simply weren't calling.

The Gators finished the regular season 8–2. Their record was good enough for them to receive an invitation to play in the Orange Bowl. This time, the great Gatorade moment was not engineered.

Prior to coming to the University of Florida, Graves had been an assistant coach at Georgia Tech for 13 years (1947–1959). Now he was facing his mentor, Bobby Dodd, whose team had won its first nine games that year. The Orange Bowl was also Dodd's final game as coach, and the game had been sold out for two months.

A crowd of 72,476 saw Florida, up only 7–6 by halftime, get its act together in the second half. Not only did Larry Smith have a 94-yard run and finish the game with 187 yards, but the Gators' defense was rock solid. Georgia Tech's quarterback, Kim King, threw four interceptions, and the Gators converted Georgia Tech's

Florida head football coach Ray Graves with his Heisman Trophy winning quarterback Steve Spurrier, who admitted to drinking Coca-Cola, not Gatorade, at halftime. (University of Florida Sports Information Department)

only fumble. Graves's men manhandled Dodd's squad, especially in the second half, outscoring the Yellow Jackets 20–6 in the third and fourth quarters.

After the game, a stunned Dodd acknowledged the Gators' advantage.

"We didn't have Gatorade," Graves said Dodd told him after the game. "That made the difference."

Despite being on the sidelines, Cade and Shires had almost no relationship with the man who may have been most responsible for the fate of Gatorade, Gators quarterback Steve Spurrier. According to the doctors, they never really talked with him. And while Spurrier could be seen drinking Gatorade on the sidelines, perhaps another drink was giving him the energy for those great second halves.

Said Spurrier: "We drank Coca-Cola at halftime of the games, because that is what they gave us."

With the season now over and no one picking up on the Gators' choice of halftime beverage, momentum was on Cade's side. He hoped that his drink could become a real commercial success. The time to grow was now. In October 1966, the doctors all of a sudden had competition on the market, although they all say that they were not aware of it. Cramer, an athletics products company out of Gardner, Kansas, sent out its brochure to athletic directors, coaches, and trainers. Amidst the Strawberry Ointment and Fung-O-Spray was a color picture of "Take 5," the company's citrus-flavored "Instant Salt Dextrose Drink" to help "replace salt and fluids lost due to excessive sweating." It was a bargain at 31 cents a gallon.

But given its story, Gatorade had a hook that no other brand had. Much-needed support came from Eugene Tubbs, who really believed that Gatorade was going to be a commercial success. Tubbs befriended the doctors during his stint in internal medicine at Florida's teaching hospital, and although he was now at Cape Canaveral, 165 miles away from Gainesville, fulfilling his Air Force requirement, Tubbs had kept up with the progress of the drink.

Believing that this gold mine had to be protected, Tubbs found a lawyer in Orlando, who began the process of registering the initial patent for the sports drink and trademarking its unique name.

Meanwhile, University of Florida coaches started spreading Gatorade throughout the state as a recruiting tool. Cade would give them Gatorade to go to high schools with, and they would present it to the coach in order to get him on their side. Cade was giving out Gatorade in the hopes that people would ask for more and pay for it. But when people did ask for more, Cade had a hard time getting paid.

Cade also "sold" 100 gallons of Gatorade to a doctor in a school district in Alhambra, California. After six weeks, Cade called to see if he had received the bill, to which the doctor replied, according to Cade, "I thought it was a gift—one doctor to another."

As had been the case with Graves, who finally relented and agreed to pay more than the cost of the ingredients to supply Gatorade for a second season, Cade was hoping that he'd get paid more often.

Actual sales to schools like the University of Richmond and Miami of Ohio yielded the doctors a meager $1,500. Since the cost of shipping out Gatorade solution would be too great, Cade and his head laboratory technician, Kelly Campbell, started putting concentrate in bottles and offering them at $15 per bottle. They even brokered a cheap deal on the shipping—putting their bottles on Greyhound buses.

In some cases, Cade would give Gatorade away for free in exchange for free publicity. Jerry Quarry was one of the best heavyweight boxers never to win a title. Quarry had just won the National Golden Gloves at Madison Square Garden, and he had a great record, but Quarry's manager had told Cade that his fighter needed Gatorade to improve his record in fights that went into the later rounds. In exchange for promoting Gatorade to others, Quarry's Gatorade allotment was free of charge.

But orders weren't flowing in, and after a couple months of being in business, Cade was beginning to speculate publicly that his great idea might die in the lab. He was happy that people were so excited about the product, but finding someone who would take on the responsibility of making and selling it was a different proposition.

"We were kind of discouraged," DeQuesada said. "None of us really had the money to support it."

If only Cade could meet the right person in the beverage industry to turn his mom-and-pop product into a booming business. Luckily, his web of colleagues was in the right place at the right time. If things hadn't fallen into place as they did, Gatorade most likely would never have gotten off the ground.

In the spring of 1966, a letter arrived in Cade's mailbox from Indiana University medical school. The university was looking for a nephrologist. At the time, neither Cade nor Shires was interested, but Kent Bradley, a general internist who had made rounds in the kidney clinics for six months, went for it and got the job.

Commercial Interest

Bradley was good at meeting and forming relationships with people. He was, by all accounts, an attractive man with a great personality. At the medical school, Bradley came in contact with Conrad Johnston, an endocrinologist at the university, whose wife's sister was married to Alfred Stokely, chairman of the board of Stokely-Van Camp. The Indianapolis-based company was famous for its canned foods, especially its Pork & Beans.

After fostering a relationship with Johnston, Bradley made his way to the company's Christmas party in 1966, where, by chance, he met Stokely and told him about the unique product made by a bunch of doctors in Gainesville.

Stokely was initially intrigued by the idea of making Gatorade. Intrigue soon turned into serious interest, thanks to the fact that the 1966–67 University of Florida basketball team was also having the greatest year in its history—and its players, too, were using Gatorade.

The team opened the season 11–1, thanks to beating Adolf Rupp's Kentucky team twice. On December 17, 1966, when the

Gators defeated the Wildcats for the first time ever in Lexington, a writer for Louisville's *Courier-Journal* wrote, "They call this stuff Gatorade, and whatever's in it, Kentucky should find out."

Thanks to all the exposure, Stokely executives were on the lookout when the Gators came to Tennessee on January 21. Although the Gators were defeated by the Volunteers in back-to-back games (handing them two of their four losses that year), the company's executives were still interested in taking a look at the drink. Gatorade had many things going for it.

CHAPTER 3

From Field to Shelves

IN MARCH 1967, Dana Shires and Kent Bradley walked into the three-story, gray concrete building at 941 North Meridian Street in downtown Indianapolis known as the Stokely-Van Camp headquarters. The building itself wasn't hard to find, as a large reddish-orange Stokely-Van Camp logo sat on the roof.

Shires and Bradley briefed the lone receptionist in the small and sparse lobby on their intentions, and the receptionist promptly called the secretary of Hank Warren, the company's vice president and director of sales and marketing.

"Two men are here," his assistant said. "They have a product. They said they met with Mr. Stokely, and they want to come in and talk about it."

Warren, an 18-year company veteran, was always open to ideas.

So he called Bob Rice, Stokely-Van Camp's national sales manager, and brought the company's lead general counsel, George "Linc" Lewis, to his office on the first floor to make sure the company would be legally protected. Shires and Bradley were brought through the lobby and walked down a long hall where members of Stokely-Van Camp's traffic department worked. They passed cubicles on their left and open offices on their right, each with a metal desk and a short gray swivel chair.

Their final destination was Warren's office—without a doubt the best corner office on the first floor. It wasn't hard for Shires and Bradley to figure out that they were in the workplace of a man who had power. Not only did Warren have a carpeted office, he had wood furniture, a huge leather couch, and a private bathroom.

Shires and Bradley sat down in chairs in the office, holding samples of their product in Ball jars. And the two began to tell their story of how their product had worked at the University of Florida.

"I couldn't believe what they had," said Warren, who was described by Stokely-Van Camp employees as a rough and demanding man who had never lost the edge after serving as a Marine during World War II. "Kent was a great communicator and really sold me on the product."

Shires had always said that Bradley was such a good salesman that he could sell ice to the Eskimos. Yes, he could even pitch Gatorade, which was still far from perfected.

"We tasted it," said Rice, who had watched Gators coach Ray Graves play for the Volunteers while serving as an usher at games during his Boy Scout years. "It was really awful."

Warren wasn't sure what the board would think, but right there on the spot, he signed a letter of intent to look at the product. They came up with a three-month exclusive negotiating window.

It helped that the Stokely family had always had a tie to the sports world. In the early 1890s, William Burnett Stokely had organized a group of football players at the University of Tennessee the year after the university's athletic association voted to drop football. His son, William Jr., also attended Tennessee and was a big fan of the team, thanks in part to the fact that his fraternity brother and roommate was Estes Kefauver, the team's offensive tackle, who would go on to become governor and running mate of presidential candidate Adlai Stevenson in 1956. William Jr. became one of the university's largest sports boosters, donating $500,000 to help upgrade the school's Armory Fieldhouse, which was later named in his honor.

William Jr. always made sure that the football team's training table was filled with Stokely-Van Camp products, including sauerkraut juice, which, like Gatorade, helped replenish salts lost during practices and games. He didn't get to see what would become one of his company's most famous products; he passed away in October 1965 at the age of 66.

By the time Shires and Bradley arrived at the company's headquarters, Stokely-Van Camp was a national power in food, fruit, and vegetable processing, with gross sales surpassing $200 million annually. The company, thanks to its invention of the Type C Ration, was one of the many organizations helped by World War II. The Type C was a box made for soldiers that included a day's worth of food, including the company's bestselling Pork & Beans, beef, and candy.

Seasonal items such as green peas, corn, and tomatoes were sold under the Stokely label, while year-round items such as the company's processed Pork & Beans and chili were called Van Camp's. The company was also making fruit juices using the Stokely name, such as Ping (pineapple-grapefruit), Pi-Li (pineapple-lime), and

Pong (pineapple-orange), which undoubtedly gave it a better chance of selling Gatorade.

In Gatorade They Trust

Gatorade wasn't really a natural fit with the company's portfolio, but the alliance did make some sense. Soft drink companies didn't sterilize their bottles because the carbonation in their drinks provided such high levels of acidity that not enough bacteria could grow in that environment. But Gatorade, of course, wasn't carbonated, and a more costly sterilization process, in which the liquid had to be heated before it was put into cans or bottles, was needed. Not only had Stokely recently decided to make the majority of its cans, but its foods and juices had to be sterilized as well, so its packing plants were already equipped to take on the task.

Things were moving forward. A few weeks prior to Shires and Bradley's meeting at Stokely headquarters, the lawyers in Orlando had filed the articles of incorporation for Gatorade Inc. in the state of Florida. The initial capital listed was $500, and the directors included the four doctors and Eugene Tubbs. By April, the corporation had trademarked the name "Gatorade."

The negotiations with Stokely were led by Claude Spilman, a well-known lawyer in Indianapolis. Spilman was introduced to the Gatorade doctors through Kent Bradley, who was dialyzing Spilman.

The doctors were finally convinced that they could make money off Gatorade. So they told Spilman that they wanted to try to get a $1 million flat fee for their product.

It wasn't going to be easy. Warren wasn't even sure that the company's management would agree to take on the drink.

The key decision makers were chairman Alfred Stokely, William B. Stokely Jr.'s cousin, and Herb Krimendahl, the company president. The sentiment among the board members was that the product didn't taste very good, and that the idea of selling to athletes only didn't really fit into the company's goal of selling to the mass market.

"There wasn't a lot of support by the board," Warren said. "But I overpowered them."

Despite Warren's pushing, the $1 million price tag wasn't going to work, since the board wasn't sure the product would ever sell.

To protect itself from making a foolish investment, the board authorized Warren to explore the possibility of a royalty structure, in which the doctors would earn a percentage of the sales.

Dave McVay, the company's financial vice president, had so little confidence in the potential of Gatorade that he told Warren that if the company were ever in a position to sell the product for at least $20,000, they should consider doing so.

Stokely's decision not to pay the $1 million fee turned out to be a boon for the doctors. Instead of collecting a couple of hundred thousand dollars each, they were to earn more than $30 million each over the next 40 years. In advance of a final agreement, Spilman set up the Gatorade Trust, signed on May 16, 1967. Cade, Shires, Free, and DeQuesada each started with 17 of the 101 total shares.

Tubbs received a 17 percent stake for his support of the project, and Bradley got 10 shares for making the connection with Stokely. Two football trainers who had originally supported the experiment, Jim Cunningham and Brady Greathouse, received a couple of shares each, and Loren Roby, a lab technician, was also included in the trust agreement. There were nine original trust members.

Warren was in close touch with Jim Keys, Stokely's attorney, who had arrived at the company two years before to serve in more of a marketing capacity. When it came time to negotiate the deal, Keys went to Cold Springs Veterans Administration Hospital. That's where he met with Spilman, who was working the entire time he was on dialysis.

"I sat there negotiating the agreement at the same time I had access to the tube that was conveying the blood from his body to the dialysis machine and back into his body," Keys said. "Now that's leverage!"

A few days later, Spilman, Keys, Tubbs, Bradley, and Shires met in Indianapolis and, in front of Stokely representatives, formally signed the documents that would give the company the exclusive world rights to manufacture, market, sell, and distribute Gatorade.

The cost?

A $5,000 signing bonus, a royalty of 5 cents on every gallon sold, and a guaranteed payout of $25,000.

Marketing Issues

The doctors had sold their product, but in order to make more money, Stokely had a couple things that it had to take care of before Gatorade hit the market.

The first was to make the product more palatable. The company assigned one of its chemists named June Davis to that task. Davis had worked on Jell-O flavors at General Foods before coming to Stokely-Van Camp. With Gatorade, she had a challenge on her hands. She couldn't sweeten the product significantly, since that would slow down the speed with which it made its way through the body.

"We knew it would never be Coca-Cola, but we had to make it better," Rice said. "You really couldn't drink the damn stuff."

In a short time, Davis came back with her changes. She added 2 percent more sugar to the solution and determined that this didn't have much effect on the speed of absorption of the liquid. She also made a number of flavors, including orange, grape, cranberry, fruit punch, and even iced tea, without changing the integrity of the product. It was a good experiment, but Warren was only interested in how she could make the original lemon-lime flavor better.

"I was very much against rolling out other flavors because the product wasn't even developed yet," said Warren, who agreed to rolling out orange Gatorade in 1969.

The next order of business was to determine whether the Gatorade name should stay. Stokely executives were concerned that some people might think that the drink had alligator juice in it, so they dreamed up 40 other names, including Thirst-Aide, Super-Star, Quench, and Rebound. But, in the end, an informal poll revealed that Gatorade was already a well-recognized brand name. To destroy the name would be to destroy its association with the university's teams, which had enjoyed such great success while using it. The decision to keep the name was to pay dividends in the near future.

The first big meeting to talk about how Gatorade would be sold was to take place in mid-July of 1967. Stokely-Van Camp was holding one of its national sales meetings at the Greenbrier Resort in White Sulphur Springs, West Virginia. Food brokers who sold Stokely-Van Camp's product to distributors across the country were scheduled to attend, and Gatorade was prominently on the agenda.

But Warren received the worst of news as he prepared for the brokers to come into town: A Piedmont Airlines plane had collided with a private plane over western North Carolina. All 74 people on the Boeing 727 were killed, including Secretary of the Navy John T.

McNaughton as well as more than 20 food brokers who worked for Stokely. It was the first of many setbacks for the Gatorade brand.

The next obstacle that Stokely executives encountered actually came just weeks later. Gatorade was originally marketed solely to sports teams, so Stokely executives decided to package the product in bulk. Each 46-ounce can of Gatorade represented approximately six servings.

Although Stokely had the sterilization process down thanks to its experience with canned foods, company officials didn't realize that Gatorade's ingredients, particularly the salts, would penetrate through the metal can and cause the drink to leak. The result was embarrassment more than anything else.

Stokely was pushing the product as hard as it could. Ed Ansel, the product marketing director for Gatorade, had already begun to send out samples to analysts on Wall Street, hoping that they would believe that the quality of the product would contribute to the company's popularity.

"One of them put the cans on the back seat of his Lincoln and left them there overnight," Ansel said. "We had to buy the guy a new back seat." Another analyst that Ansel sent a case to left it on his walnut desk. Stokely officials replaced the desk.

Luckily, the unfortunate learning experience didn't seem to affect the analysts' opinions, as they gave the product glowing reviews. In four months' time, Stokely's stock price doubled—a result that was directly attributed to Gatorade.

The disintegration of the cans forced the marketers at Stokely to shift their retail product to 32-ounce glass bottles. Gatorade soon was being produced in glass bottles, which of course presented another problem. Stokely executives were soon finding out how right the philosopher Plato was in *The Republic*, when he stated that necessity "is the mother of invention."

Sports teams didn't want athletes to have to deal with glass, so Stokely had to create something that would enable the teams to make the product themselves. The result was a pouch of powdered concentrate that would make a gallon of Gatorade when mixed with water.

The company had to make a lot of those pouches. In a year's time, Stokely had managed to sell Gatorade to almost 2,000 organizations, from teams to schools to country clubs. It was just the beginning, and the stories kept coming.

Ara Parseghian's Notre Dame football team was reportedly a holdout, which was not good for Stokely because it wanted to have the product in the hands of the players who had won the national championship the year before. Notre Dame changed its mind shortly after the team was beaten by the Purdue Boilermakers in West Lafayette, Indiana, on September 30, 1967.

The Irish at the time were the number one–ranked team in the nation and were led by future Pittsburgh Steelers running back Rocky Bleier. Purdue was ranked 10th and had running back Leroy Keyes, who finished third in the Heisman Trophy voting that year. But the team's All-American Bob Griese had graduated the year before, after engineering a 14-13 victory over Kellen Winslow and the USC Trojans in the Rose Bowl.

Purdue was an easy Gatorade customer. Not only did many Purdue alumni work for Stokely, but the school's campus was only 65 miles from Stokely-Van Camp headquarters (Notre Dame was 145 miles away). As legend has it, just two days after the 28-21 victory by the Boilermakers, a Notre Dame team representative who was aware of the drink disparity that day ordered 20 cases of Gatorade.

Gatorade was such a dynamic product that when the media inquired, Gatorade drinkers and customers would swear by it without any prompting from Stokely.

"We had something similar made up in our lab last season, but the players prefer the commercial stuff," Army coach Tom Cahill told the *Miami Herald* in November 1967. "Does it help? They think so. And I'm for anything that gives my team a psychological lift."[1]

Cahill was the first to suggest that Gatorade was perhaps good for his players' mental state. Maybe the drink didn't actually do anything, but if his players believed it did, they would play better.

This phenomenon is referred to in the medical industry as the placebo effect.

"If you told a football player that you were giving him Demerol to relieve pain and you gave him a placebo instead, there's about a 30 percent chance that the placebo will relieve the pain as much as taking Demerol would have," Dr. Cade said.

It might not have been clear why teams were buying Gatorade, but what was clear throughout this early period was that Gatorade was on a roll.

NFL Coolers and Cups

Some of the credit for this goes to Stokely executives, who, in 1967, had had the foresight to sign a $25,000-a-year deal to be called the official sports drink of the NFL. They then capitalized on this relationship by making the general public aware of what the players were drinking through the use of coolers and cups with the Gatorade logo on them. When negotiating the agreement, Jim Keys had the idea of putting in the contract that all NFL teams would have to put coolers on their sidelines for every game. Teams weren't required to drink Gatorade, however, and some teams didn't buy it, because they still had to pay for it.

The coolers, with Gatorade decals on them, came about because college and professional teams were making huge volumes of the drink and needed something that they could put the powder and water in and then mix them. Stokely-Van Camp executives contacted a cooler maker and ordered orange buckets with white tops. When teams bought a certain amount of Gatorade, they received points, which could then be redeemed for free jugs.

The green waxed-paper cups that have been so closely connected with the Gatorade brand over the years were the brainchild of a young marketing intern named Jay Funderberg. One day, Funderberg, who also made calls pitching Gatorade to teams, decided to order 50,000 cups so that he could include the item as a throw-in when teams ordered Gatorade. Funderberg understood that if teams used cups with the Gatorade logo emblazoned on them, it would give Gatorade even better exposure than the coolers, which were sitting on the ground. But when the head of Stokely's promotions department, Bob Richey, found out about the order, which would cost the company thousands of dollars, Funderberg almost got fired. He ultimately survived, and, luckily, so did the idea.

In addition to the ingenuity on the part of Stokely executives, the product seemed to market itself pretty well.

Although not every NFL team was using it religiously, those players on teams that were would swear by it.

Said offensive lineman Jerry Kramer of the Green Bay Packers, who won the first two Super Bowls in 1966 and 1967: "If the Packers stop buying it for the whole team, I'll go out and buy it myself out of my own pocket."[2]

Although Gatorade wasn't yet available to the public in Alabama in November 1967, people were well aware of the product. On November 4, the Florida Gators took on the Auburn Tigers on the road at Cliff Hare Stadium, and the cover of the game program that day featured a cartoon of an alligator tied up, while the Tigers' tiger mascot, Aubie, was burping from drinking "vitamin-enriched Gatorade." The jug also mentioned that it was the Gators' "entire supply for the Auburn game"—no doubt a play on the Georgia tale.

The public may have known about Gatorade, but Stokely executives weren't completely convinced that the product had mass appeal. Anyone who inquired about purchasing Gatorade directly from the company usually backed off from the request after hearing how much it would cost. For $3.90, they could buy twelve 46-ounce cans. But the package weighed so much the shipping cost was an exorbitant $30 per case.

Early advertising dollars were spent in publications like the *Athletic Journal*, which went to teams and trainers.

"We can drink all the Gatorade we want, all through the game," read an ad in the publication featuring Chicago White Sox pitchers Joel Horlen and Gary Peters, who won a combined 35 games for the team in 1967.

It was becoming more and more important for Stokely to advertise in publications like these. Gatorade's success with teams had given rise to more competitors. Cramer's Take 5 and Becton Dickinson's Sportade were soon joined by Half-Time Punch. Even a man training for the 1968 U.S. Olympic Trials tried his hand at making his own sports drink—Bill Gookin's Gookinaid still exists today.

In the summer of 1968, at the same time that it sent out 31,000 samples of Gatorade to athletic programs across the country, Stokely began rolling out Gatorade in supermarkets. One quart of Gatorade was soon selling for 39 cents in Jacksonville, Tampa, and Miami, Florida.

It was perfect timing yet again. The government was embarking on a national effort to educate Americans on the benefits of vigorous activity, and those who were already exercising tried Gatorade and always seemed to be enthusiastic about it, giving it credit for their performance.

Mary Row, a mother of five, won a 22-mile amateur bicycle race in Miami. The second-place finisher was drinking beet juice. When asked where her energy came from, Row credited the apple she ate and the Gatorade for pushing her to the finish line.

Success in test markets was surprising. Every Monday morning, selected Stokely representatives would hear from brokers how sales had gone for the week. Those numbers were brought to the 1 p.m. meeting of the marketing committee. Mark Newberry, the company's vice president of marketing, was so pleased with the numbers that he eventually made plans for unveiling the product in every major city within a year's time. By October 1968, Gatorade was on shelves in "winter markets" such as Cleveland, Kansas City, and Stokely's hometown of Indianapolis.

Sports Illustrated

People in those markets now knew what Gatorade was, thanks in part to an article by Gil Rogin that appeared in the July 1 issue of *Sports Illustrated* that year. It wasn't that someone managing Stokely's advertising account or public relations group had pitched the piece; it was yet another unplanned coup for the brand that continued to be rewarded for being unique.

"Famous athletic teams rave over a cloudy, lime-green liquid with some strange attributes and an unfamiliar taste,"[3] read the text leading into the six-and-a-half-page story. In the piece, Rogin sang Gatorade's praises.

Rogin cited statistics that were meant to back up the claim that Gatorade worked for the Gators. Since the team began drinking

Gatorade, it had outscored its opponents in the second half by a 379–221 margin. In the first half, Florida's margin was only 290–204. And Rogin collected quotes from the biggest names in sports, who spoke about Gatorade in the nation's most popular sports magazine as if they had been paid to do so. It might have not happened if Keys had not recently negotiated a deal with the National Basketball Association (NBA).

"I'd like to think Gatorade gives me more stamina and endurance," Los Angeles Lakers forward Elgin Baylor said. "I can't prove it, but as long as I continue to feel it does me some good, I'll continue to drink it."[4]

Said teammate Jerry West, whose silhouette eventually became the NBA logo: "I drink it like mad during a game. Since I've used it, I never get that real tired, totally exhausted feeling you get in a pressure game. If I had that much water in me I couldn't walk, let alone run."

After the article, calls flowed in to Stokely headquarters, just as they had in Gainesville following Amdur's piece in the *Miami Herald*.

And it wasn't just anyone. Athletes themselves were calling.

"Gatorade hit at a particular time in our cultural history where people started to realize that the use of nutritional supplements was crucial to performance," said sports sociologist Jay Coakley. "At the very least this was the first performance enhancer that was marketed openly, and it was at a time when people were primed to connect science with performance."

Unlike Dr. Cade, who was so excited about his product that he initially gave it away for free in exchange for the publicity, Stokely executives were told that no matter who called, they had to pay for it.

The orders came from E. J. Mooney, Stokely's new products manager, who said that his everyone-had-to-buy-it philosophy not only would be fiscally responsible, but would also help to build Gatorade's mystique. After all, magic potions rarely come gratis.

A call came into Stokely headquarters one day. The person calling was transferred to Ed Ansel. He answered the phone.

"Hi, this is Arthur Ashe, and I need some Gatorade for the Davis Cup team."

Ashe was on his way to becoming a household name. He had won many amateur championships and was considered the best young tennis player in the country. He had played on the Davis Cup team since 1963 and was months away from becoming the first African American to win a singles championship—he won the U.S. Open in September of 1968. Ashe was shocked when he was told that his team would have to pay for Gatorade.

"I understand that this is the Davis Cup team, Mr. Ashe, but we don't give Gatorade away for free," Ansel said. Ashe eventually relented and ordered about $800 of the product.

By November 1968, Cade was gloating, saying that he expected that he and his Gatorade Trust could one day expect to make up to $2.5 million a year in royalties. Comments like this made it sound as if he was proud of the fact that the product he had invented was soon going to be padding his bank account. But there was never any evidence to show that Cade was particularly enamored with money. Out of the first $60,000 he received from Gatorade, the only money he spent was $400 on a sofa. Millions eventually did flow in, and Cade gave much of his earnings from the product to charities and scholarships. When he talked about how much money his product would be earning, it was his way of expressing his pride in how successful his product would one day become.

By 1969, Gatorade's national rollout was in full force. Stokely executives made presentations to wholesalers and supermarket managers, explaining how the product worked, in order to generate interest and hopefully lead them to order the product. Stokely insisted that the product not be placed with the colas to avoid consumer confusion. Instead, it sat in supermarkets next to artificial juices such as Hi-C and Kool-Aid. Stokely licensed Gatorade in a sparkling form to Royal Crown in order to try to use the growing Gatorade brand name in the soda category.

By June 1969, Gatorade had become the pride and joy of the Stokely brand. It was the company's new Pork & Beans. Stokely had rolled out Gatorade in 32 cities, including New York, and was on the cusp of beginning a $4 million advertising campaign—the most Stokely had ever spent on a single campaign for one of its brands.

Gatorade was advertised as "The Big Thirst Quencher" that was made "for active people everywhere."

"Now available for thirsty kids, thirsty moms, thirsty dads," read an ad in the *Washington Post*, which also tried to impress athletes by pointing to the company's relationship with the NFL and a newly formed alliance with Major League Baseball.

Stokely hired Coach Graves, who was coaching for his last year at Florida, to appear in television commercials with players whose eligibility had expired.

Stokely was so eager to push Gatorade's sales that some of those managing the brand almost pushed it too far. One advertising executive tried to convince Stokely counsel Jim Keys that the company should tout Gatorade as a lifesaver.

"He wanted us to make an ad that said, 'If you don't drink Gatorade while exercising, you can possibly die,'" Keys said. "We couldn't do that."

One of Gatorade's earliest advertisements did appear in *Playboy*, of all places. The ad, featuring bottles with beads of sweat on them, read, "Gatorade: It can take care of any kind of thirst you can work up. Any kind."

Stokely's stockholders weren't happy, and Gatorade was never advertised in *Playboy* again. It was a momentary slip, but it wasn't going to stop the momentum that the brand had.

Despite all the focus Stokely placed on advertising on television and in magazines and newspapers, its greatest advertisements continued to be the endorsements that came out of the blue, from the most unexpected people.

"Actors in the Broadway production 'Hair' say it beats LSD," wrote a reporter for *Newsweek*. "It is, in fact, one of the hottest new products to hit the U.S. in years, with a potential market that may go well beyond sports."[5]

Just ask Elvis.

From July 31 to August 28, 1969, just as Stokely was rolling out its advertising campaign, Elvis Presley performed 57 shows at the International Hotel in Las Vegas. Presley's drink of choice, which he had next to him on the stage, was Gatorade.

In between songs, Elvis would talk to his fans about things he was into—like his black belt in karate, for example—and Gatorade was a part of that.

"They give this stuff to athletes," Elvis said. "It's supposed to work twelve times faster than water. It looks like it's already been used to me."[6]

"He gulped it down in front of his fans like his life depended on it," said Elvis historian Crister Berge, who has written countless articles reviewing Elvis's work. "And when he got into something, it spread around the world pretty quickly."

In the concert documentary *That's the Way It Is: Special Edition* (1970), Elvis is seen holding a bottle while he sings a song.

Berge said that in many performances between 1969 and 1974, Elvis mentioned the sports drink.

"He always said, 'This is Gatorade—in case you want to aid your gator,'" Burge said.

Nothing could stop Gatorade. Or so it was thought.

In October 1969, Stokely was preparing to reintroduce Gatorade in cans in the test market of Jacksonville. The new 12-ounce cans had a special lining so that the ingredients wouldn't leak through as they had before. But a couple of weeks before the launch, Stokely executives heard the worst of news—their golden product was about to face a significant battle for survival.

Cyclamate Disaster

When the University of Florida doctors were formulating Gatorade, their only sugar was the nonsweet glucose. But Cade and the others realized that they needed another sugar substitute that would help the product taste better.

One day, Cade went upstairs to a faculty member in the College of Pharmacy and asked him to suggest an artificial sweetener that could be put in the product, but that would not slow down the way the original formula made its way through the body. The artificial sweetener the faculty member suggested was calcium cyclamate.

At the time, cyclamate (an odorless white powder) worked particularly well for Cade because it was about 30 times sweeter than sugar and, perhaps even more important, was less expensive.

Cyclamate was invented by accident in 1937 by a scientist named Michael Sveda. According to legend, Sveda was smoking a cigarette and put it down on a pile of powder he was experimenting with. When he picked it up, he noticed a sweet taste; thus cyclamate was born.

It started to be used as a food additive in 1958, and over a 10-year period, the substance came to be used in a huge part of the diet food and drink industry, which had grown into a $1 billion business, thanks to Americans becoming conscious of counting their calories.

By 1969, approximately 15 million pounds of the sweetener were used by about 175 million Americans in approximately 250 products, ranging from desserts and canned foods to diet drinks.

The Food and Drug Administration (FDA) of the U.S. Department of Health and Human Services administers the Federal Food, Drug and Cosmetic Act of 1938. This act makes the FDA responsible for ensuring the quality of products and food additives sold in the United States. Under the Delaney clause in the Food Additive Amendment, which was added 20 years later, it became the FDA's responsibility to take a substance off the market if it was found to induce cancer in an animal or in humans.

As early as 1950, an FDA doctor had noted that studies of cyclamate in rats revealed frequent lung tumors. Various lab tests throughout the 1950s and 1960s provided further warnings. But cyclamate remained on the FDA's Generally Recognized As Safe (GRAS) list.

In 1968, FDA biochemist Dr. Jacqueline Verrett injected cyclamate into chicken eggs. Her study revealed an unusually high rate of birth deformities in the embryos. Verrett's studies continued throughout the following year, but the results remained out of the public eye until October of 1969, when Verrett went on national television and showed the deformities in chickens that had been injected with the sweetener in the egg. She presented her findings on *NBC Nightly News*.

While this very public presentation led to a national scare over cyclamate, the majority of viewers who watched the show were unaware of Verrett's testing methods. In order to simulate the effect on a large population, scientists frequently take a smaller sample of subjects, but increase the dosage. The problem with this is that the resulting exposure is at a level that would never occur in humans.

To make a point, a few days after the airing of Verrett's findings, the largest maker of cyclamate, Abbott Laboratories, released a study that showed that 8 of 240 rats fed a mixture of saccharin and cyclamate developed bladder tumors. The amount of the mixture used, however, was equivalent to a human ingesting 350 cans of diet soda each day. The general population was perhaps also not aware of the outside pressure on cyclamate coming from the sugar industry, which was being undersold by cyclamate. From 1964 through 1969, the sugar industry reportedly pumped $500,000 into research on cyclamate.

Though it was unlikely that humans would consume enough cyclamate to be dangerous, this didn't calm the fears of the buying public. Consumers feared the worst. On Friday, October 17, 1969, in a preemptive move, Canada Dry announced that it was voluntarily pulling its products with cyclamate off the shelves throughout the world.

The next day, Robert H. Finch, secretary of Health and Human Services, in a suit and tie and with slicked-back black hair, stood at a podium in Washington, D.C., and announced that cyclamate would be removed from the list of substances generally recognized as safe for use in foods.

Soft drinks with cyclamate had to be pulled off the market by January 1, and other products had to be removed by the following month. This order was given despite the fact that at the very same press conference, Dr. Jesse Steinfeld, deputy assistant secretary for health and scientific affairs, told the media that there was no indication that cyclamate had resulted in increased cancer risk among humans.

"A 3 percent salt solution will kill you too, if you drink too much of it," cyclamate creator Michael Sveda told the *New York Times* after the announcement of the ban. "They should have tried to find out what effect massive doses of sugar would have on rats, too."[7]

The reaction in the beverage industry was swift and immediate. It had to be.

Abbott said that it would suspend the manufacture of cyclamate. Coca-Cola halted distribution of its two sodas that contained cyclamate, Tab and Fresca, and announced that newly formulated products would be on their way to supermarket shelves in no time. Pepsi placed an ad in the Sunday *New York Times* proclaiming that its new formulas without cyclamates would taste better.

On the first day of trading following the announcement, all the soft drink stocks plummeted. Among the largest losers were Abbott, which plummeted $6\frac{1}{2}$ points, and Stokely-Van Camp, which went down 4 points to $29\frac{1}{8}$ a share.[8]

The cyclamate news was a shock to executives at Stokely-Van Camp. They didn't have the resources to produce another formula and have the product back in stores quickly.

Dana Shires was driving home from Florida to Indianapolis when he heard on the radio that the FDA had banned cyclamate. He called his lawyer and patient, Claude Spilman, who set up a meeting with Stokely's lead attorney, Jim Keys. They met at Spilman's home.

Keys told Shires and Spilman that it was in the doctors' best interest to help reformulate the product that the company had spent so much money advertising. The process of pulling all the Gatorade with cyclamate in it off the market alone would cost the company more than $500,000.

Executives at Stokely were concerned that there wouldn't be a sweetener that could make the product taste good and still allow the product to move through the body as it did with cyclamate. With the help of the doctors, Vig Babayan, vice president of product development for Stokely, oversaw the reformulation of Gatorade. Cyclamates were eliminated, and some of the glucose was replaced with fructose, a simple sugar that is found in fruit and tastes very sweet, but (in small amounts) doesn't slow down the transport of the fluid into the body.

Although the cyclamate issue didn't signal the end of Gatorade, it did contribute to the downfall of one of its partners. "Royal Crown's Gatorade was the best-tasting cola I had ever had," Keys said. "But they couldn't get the same taste after cyclamate was banned."

An attempt was made. When the reformulated carbonated Gatorade was re-released, Royal Crown executives elected to put on the cans that the new product contained "No Cyclamates."

But two years later, Royal Crown, unable to make the finances work, cancelled production of the drink. Route salespeople like James Buchanan, who worked in Idaho Falls, Idaho, were informed that they could take as much Gatorade soda as they wanted, and thousands of the product's green caps were brought to the dumpster.

Unlike Royal Crown's cans, Stokely executives decided not to advertise to the public that the original product had had the banned sweetener.[9]

"We did some research and found out that only 13 percent knew that Gatorade had cyclamate to begin with," Ansel said. "So we figured we didn't want to tell the other 87 percent that it did."

A new product would be on the shelves in three months. In the meantime, the Gatorade legend continued.

Continuing the Legend

Early in Gatorade's history, Ray Graves called his colleague Hank Stram, who was coaching the Kansas City Chiefs at the time. When Stram told him that his team was having trouble practicing in the heat, Graves recommended the drink.

Chiefs defensive end Jerry Mays would typically lose more than 15 pounds during a game and had such bad cramps during a preseason game against the Rams that he needed to get saline solution injected into his legs.

Chiefs Hall of Fame linebacker and center E. J. Holub had his problems as well.

"In the preseason I passed out in the huddle, and Coach Stram knew it was from dehydration," Holub said. "We thought we had to be tough guys, but the heat was too much. The next day, we had Gatorade at practice. We were always looking for something to better our playing ability, and it was refreshing to us at the time. We didn't pass out any more."

"When our team started using Gatorade we noticed a great improvement in their endurance and there was less dehydration and loss of weight," said Chiefs trainer Wayne Rudy. "Our medical doctors felt this was a very big plus and the players were playing longer and harder."[10]

Despite the cyclamate disaster, a newly formulated Gatorade was ready in a month and was distributed to the NFL sidelines before the Chiefs went on to win Super Bowl IV that year. The connection would be immortalized in a Gatorade commercial 33 years later.

The new Gatorade hit the shelves in January and, in no time, captured the number-one market share position. Stokely was back, and it introduced an icon that would soon become synonymous with the Gatorade brand—the lightning bolt. Its origin is unclear, but its symbolism is well understood: It represented the speed of Gatorade's absorption into the body.

None of the other sports drinks available (there were more than 15 brands) stood for anything besides the teams they represented. The Georgia Bulldogs' concoction, Bulldog Punch, was available to the public, as was LSU's Bengal Punch, which was renamed Quickick. However, at best, these drinks were local successes in areas where loyalty for a particular school's team was strong.

In August of 1970, Coca-Cola announced that it would enter the fray with Olympade, a sports drink with a can draped in the colors of the American flag. Its campaign was: "If you've got a thirst for winning, you've got a thirst for Olympade."

Coca-Cola's entry proved that the sports drink market for the general public was bigger than had initially been thought. If Stokely executives were able to resist the onslaught and remain the market leader, Gatorade's inventors could look forward to collecting healthy royalties. But with millions of dollars on the line, officials with the University of Florida and the U.S. and state governments weren't going to let the scientists, who had been working under grants, have the invention and the payouts to themselves.

CHAPTER 4

Wrestling Over Gatorade

GATORADE had turned into a blue-chip brand, but all was not well between Dr. Cade and the University of Florida.

In December 1966, the first article on Gatorade was published in papers all over the country. Four days later, Cade was urged by an executive at the University of Florida to report his invention— more than fourteen months after it had been conceived.

Not realizing the ramifications, Cade filled out a form in which he declared, by default, that Gatorade was invented under a National Institutes of Health grant that he had been given in order to study sodium levels in the kidneys of rats. Over a five-year period, the NIH had given Cade more than $80,000 to perform his research.

A month later, the U.S. government informed Cade that since his work had been done under its grant, it might not be his to patent.

Yet, shortly after receiving a letter specifying the government's potential ownership of the product, Cade was part of a group that incorporated Gatorade.

Cade and the others—unbeknownst to the University of Florida or government officials—then formed the Gatorade Trust and agreed to sell their product to Stokely-Van Camp.

It was all internal business between Cade and the school until April 1968, when Cade went to speak at the Gator Boosters Club of Clearwater, where fellow Gatorade inventor Jim Free had just started up a practice.

Gatorade was on its way to becoming a major success story, as the product was starting to get a cult following among professional athletes. After Cade's talk, a question-and-answer session took place, in which some members of the media were involved. One reporter asked Cade how much money Gatorade was making and where the funds were being directed.

"I don't know how much," Cade answered. "But the money I'm making from Gatorade is several times more than the salary I'm making at the university."

The reporter followed Cade's response by asking what the university was making from the product.

"Nothing," Cade said, explaining that he had offered the product to the university, but the university had passed on the offer. "And that's exactly what they deserve."[1]

Cade was an ingenious man, but he wasn't exactly the most diplomatic in situations like this. He probably should have been thankful for the fact the University of Florida didn't have a piece of his invention, instead of chastising the university for not taking it. But he was a typical eccentric, and he had gained a reputation for sometimes speaking before he thought about the ramifications of his words.

Although Cade and the others were collecting money from Stokely on the royalties from the sales, their newfound fortune quickly became a nuisance, especially for Cade, because he was the only one still at the University of Florida. Free had moved to Clearwater, and Dana Shires and Alex DeQuesada had followed Kent Bradley to the University of Indiana in Indianapolis, where they could engage in a relationship with Stokely-Van Camp.

After Cade's appearance in Clearwater, the calls started coming into his office. Reporters and university officials were trying to understand how the school had committed the blunder of letting the scientists get away with selling Gatorade on their own. Over the course of the next three years, the Gatorade story became front-page news, and many people in the media owed a lot to Cade, who was an incredible quote machine.

"Sometimes I'm sorry I ever invented the thing," Cade told *Scientific Research* magazine in January 1968. "If Gatorade didn't get any publicity or make any money, no one would care about it. Now everybody is interested. I got a letter from a fellow who says he invented Gatorade in 1943 and is going to sue me. My lawyers tell me that if the drink is successful, I can expect to get sued two or three times a year from now on."[2]

George Sullivan wasn't suing, but he was definitely taking some credit for the Gatorade idea. In 1964 (the year before Gatorade was conceived), Sullivan said, a doctor from the University of Florida came to watch what they were doing on the sidelines at the University of Nebraska, where Sullivan was the trainer. Sullivan had been putting salt pills in water and flavoring the solution with Kool-Aid to make it more palatable; he called the product Huskerade. Cade said that he never went to Lincoln, Nebraska, to see the drink, but to this day, Sullivan still says, "In my heart I know I had a part in Gatorade."

Huskerade was never developed. Gatorade was. And when news got out that the university wasn't getting a piece of the pie, school officials had a lot of explaining to do.

The University Loses Out

By October 1968, fact finders from the state attorney's office in Tallahassee were being sent to Gainesville to investigate what had happened with Gatorade. The board of regents commissioned its own report. Files were opened; documents were pulled; people who might have been involved were questioned.

On October 25, 1968, an Associated Press article disclosed details of the lapses that had allowed Gatorade to slip through the hands of the University of Florida. Dr. Vincent Learned, the head of sponsored research, who had now left, had refused to fund the product without telling all the university administrators, and there was no written document explaining Learned's decision.

"The university at the time—by omission, I suppose—decided to let it go," said Dr. Emanuel Suter, dean of the medical school. "In 99.99 percent of cases, nothing marketable comes from research. No one could know of the tremendous demand for Gatorade."[3]

To compound matters, Cade didn't sign an invention waiver form that he was supposed to sign as part of his contract papers for the 1966–67 school year. This form was essential to giving the university the right to ascertain its interest in products developed by its professors.

At newspapers across the state of Florida, copy editors wrote the headlines on a story that was surely just beginning.

The Tallahassee Democrat: "Nationwide Scandal Brews on Gatorade Drink."

The St. Petersburg Times: "Gatorade: The Success That Ran Away."

The Tampa Tribune: "Public Funds Helped Develop Gatorade, But Taxpayers Lose Out."

The Orlando Sentinel: "Who Really Owns Gatorade?"

The Pensacola Journal: "Battle Shapes for Gatorade Bonanza; $2 Million Yearly Sales Seen."

Cade truly believed that the university had missed its chance. He felt he owed it nothing, as all four of the doctors had used only their personal time (approximately 150 hours of it) to develop the product.

The government appeared to have a stronger case because Cade not only had reported Gatorade as a product of its grant, but also admitted to using $42 worth of supplies (in the form of radioactive sulfate to measure the extracellular fluid volumes in the players) that were earmarked for the research covered by the grant. Cade countered by saying that sodium levels in the kidney of a rat and Gatorade's premise of speeding up absorption of salt and sugar in the human small intestine were two completely different areas.

"I think it's involuntary servitude, which is a violation of the Constitution," Cade said. "It applies to me the same as it did slaves after the Civil War."[4]

Despite having a weaker case, it was the university that fought Cade the hardest over the next two years. Lawyers for the university and the Gatorade Trust exchanged letters back and forth. As the profits from the Gatorade brand rose, the university's claim to the product actually became more relevant.

University of Florida president Stephen O'Connell knew that Gatorade was able to gain publicity because it was tied to the success of the University of Florida football team. The university had given the doctors the chance to put their product on a national stage every Saturday. If the Gators hadn't done well while using Gatorade, it would have been highly unlikely that the drink would have made it out of the laboratory.

It was also pretty hard to miss the fact that Stokely-Van Camp was capitalizing on the drink's association with the school. The earliest television commercials for the product didn't feature actors, they featured former Gators football players Harmon Wages, Tommy Hungerbuhler, and Don Giordano, as well as head coach Ray Graves.

Commercial Voice-over: This is a laboratory. That's right, a laboratory. Where scientists working with the Florida Gators developed the greatest thirst invention since water. "Gatorade, The Big Thirst Quencher For Active People!"

"The wide advertising of Gatorade is undoubtedly due in part to the fact that much of the advertising implies endorsement by the University," O'Connell wrote to Dr. Manuel Hiller, assistant general counsel for the government's Department of Health and Human Services, which had funded Cade's grant. "Those responsible for the marketing clearly recognize this, as evidenced by advertising on television which used football players who ostensibly were members of the Florida football team as well as the actual coach of the Florida team. The university cannot, therefore be disassociated from the product 'Gatorade.'"[5]

Cade largely refused to cooperate with the investigation. He didn't return phone calls, and, when he was reached, he would not talk about the trust's arrangement with Stokely-Van Camp. He was upset about how he was being treated.

By January 1969, he just wanted to move on. He offered to give his entire share in the trust (13 percent; he had already given away four shares) to the school.

"I felt sorry for the University of Florida," Cade said. "Press reports made them look sloppy."[6]

It was estimated at the time that 13 percent of the trust could eventually be valued at $2.6 million, but university officials, believing that they could possibly wind up with more, rejected the offer.

The Trust Takes It to Court

The trust's lawyer, Claude Spilman, was uncomfortable with the university's continuing threats to sue the doctors for a share of Gatorade. He believed that if the University of Florida precipitated the action, the case would be heard in Florida, where practically all the judges were University of Florida graduates. So on January 2, 1970, Spilman filed a motion for declaratory judgment in Indianapolis, Stokely-Van Camp's home, where a favorable outcome was more likely.

"Gatorade started out as fun," Cade told the *Atlanta Journal-Constitution*. "A lark, just a little probe into man's machinery. It's not a joke anymore. There's a lot of money involved."

The university was doing its own mobilizing. An article in *Chemical Week* seemed to confirm to members of the board of regents that the thirst-quencher market could one day be worth hundreds of millions. They knew they could not let this go.

By January 1970, Cade had collected $42,000 from the trust, and as Gatorade sales increased, the public fury over the university's not getting a cut mounted. As a result of the civil action that had been filed, the doctors' money was held in escrow until all legal proceedings were completed and the rightful owner of Gatorade had been decided.

Cade was jaded by the battle. In March 1970, he announced that he would leave the University of Florida for a school that would treat him better.

"I've learned several things about people as a result of this," Cade told the *Wall Street Journal.* "One, everybody is greedy. Whenever a considerable amount of money is involved, whoever thinks he had anything to do with it wants a share."[7]

The threat of Cade's leaving didn't do anything for the case. Perhaps university officials believed that in time the trust would fold. The doctors' legal fees had risen to $100,000 by July 1971.

"And the university thought these doctors were driving up to their big mansions in pigskin Mercedes cars," said James Dressler, lawyer for Eugene Tubbs, a member of the trust.

Cade Explodes

With no settlement in sight, the University of Florida filed suit in Florida against the trust and Stokely-Van Camp in July 1971.

Reporters couldn't reach Cade because he was in Munich, Germany, at the International Physiological Society meeting presenting a paper on ammonia. But shortly after he returned, the U.S. government filed suit in Washington, D.C., and a reporter for the *St. Petersburg Times* got his reaction.

Cade was leaving his favorite restaurant when the reporter walked up to him. According to Cade, the reporter told him that Chester Ferguson, the chairman of the board of regents, had called him "a conniving thief who had lied to the university so he could steal millions of dollars."

This comment infuriated Cade. So the learned Cade threw out a line that he remembered from *Oliver Twist*, in which Charles Dickens's character Mr. Bumble was arguing with a man and said, "If the law supposes that, the law is a ass—a idiot."

Cade told the reporter that his feelings about the board of regents were as those expressed by Mr. Bumble. His comment was printed the next day.

O'Connell wanted Cade fired for his comments. But the dean of the medical school spoke up for Cade and saved his job.

When Cade returned home that day, television crews from ABC, CBS, and NBC were camped outside his house, along with reporters from across the state. For the first time since the battle started, they were holding up microphones he didn't want to talk to. The next day, it became clear that the colorful Cade would begin a silent period.

"While I have the right to my personal opinion, I also respect the opinions and actions of others," he said, in a statement. "I wish to indicate that the statements attributed to me concerning this legal dispute regarding agencies and officials were oversimplified and resulted in inappropriate and unfortunate quotations. I do not intend to offer any further opinion or statement on this matter until a legal decision has been reached."[8]

Over the course of the next few months, the government eventually gave in because the doctors had promised to publish what Gatorade consisted of in a medical journal; thus its public duty was satisfied and a patent wasn't needed.

"We had no problem giving up the patent rights; Stokely still had the product," said Hank Warren. If Stokely had to give up the trademark, though, that would have been the end of it. As long as

Stokely had the trademark, a competing sports drink could copy Gatorade's formula exactly, but it couldn't use the Gatorade name.

The suit between the university and the doctors continued until July 1972.

It's All Settled

Dr. Dana Shires just happened to be in Atlanta for a conference on the U.S. government's funding of research projects. At the meeting was a U.S. congressman from Florida named Paul G. Rogers. Rogers had recently been appointed chair of the House Subcommittee on Health and the Environment. Shires called Spilman and told him that perhaps, given Rogers's power in the state and in Congress, he could influence a settlement.

Sure enough, a few days later, Shires and Spilman traveled to Washington, D.C., where a settlement was tentatively reached. In order to satisfy the government, the doctors had to promise to publish their findings about Gatorade. Stokely, which was allowed to keep the trademark for Gatorade, was required to abandon all three U.S. patent applications filed for the product. The University of Florida received a 20 percent share of the royalties, which included $237,509 in back pay.

Forty-five members of the trust, which had grown to 46 members by now, quickly signed off on the agreement, which needed unanimous approval. Eugene Tubbs was the lone holdout.

"He told me that he didn't have a damn thing when this thing started," said Tubbs's lawyer Jim Dressler. "And we tried to give it to those bastards and they didn't want it. So he was willing to continue fighting it, but Judge [William] Steckler ordered us to nod our heads contrary to what the agreement says."

All told, from start to finish, the battle lasted five years. The inventors had kept the majority of their rights, and while the university got the piece of the pie it was looking for, some were still unsatisfied.

"When the puny 20 percent victory was announced the other day, university officials appeared elated—which we interpret as meaning anybody will celebrate anything, even a bargain of used dental floss," wrote the staff of the *Gainesville Sun* in an editorial.[9]

On October 3, 2004, things had come full circle for Robert Cade when he received the Honorary Alumnus Award for his 43 years of service to the University of Florida's College of Medicine. That day, he was honored at halftime of the Gators football game against the Arkansas Razorbacks and received a Gators jersey with "Dr. Cade" on the back.

Despite the legal fight that had ended 32 years before, the university owed a lot to Cade and the three others who had been the faces behind Gatorade. By the end of 2004, the total of the 20 percent royalty that the University of Florida had won in 1972 was approaching $100 million.

CHAPTER 5

The "Tipping" Point

ON A WARM August night in 2003, Wagener-Salley High School football coach Steve DeRiggs never thought he would get the chills.

After a 12-game losing streak that extended back to October of 2001, the seniors who played on his high school team had almost forgotten what winning felt like. But they hadn't forgotten how every important victory should be celebrated.

Following the War Eagles' 34–0 victory, DeRiggs's players gave him something that every coach has now come to expect, yet can't evade, after that big win. Call it a dunk, a bath, a splash, or a shower, but almost all important wins are accompanied by a coach getting soaked.

Over nearly two decades, the dumping of the Gatorade cooler on the coach has become a tradition at every level of sports. During every fall weekend, a Gatorade dunking probably happens on a football field in every state, and the reporting of the event gives the brand thousands of free media mentions and impressions every year. It has reached a point where coaches in all sports—including tennis, basketball, soccer, and baseball—have received the ice-cold shower.

Stokely, and with it Gatorade, was acquired by Quaker in 1983, but had William B. Stokely III been in charge of the brand during this period, he probably would have counted each and every Gatorade dunk, just like he used to count the appearances of the cooler and cups on the NFL sidelines in the early 1980s.

The Inaugural Dunk

What happened at Wagener-Salley in South Carolina would not have occurred if New York Giants nose guard Jim Burt hadn't decided to seek revenge on his coach, Bill Parcells, in 1985.

The Giants were 3–3 that year, and Parcells, leading up to a game against the archrival Washington Redskins, was trying to motivate Burt.

"The whole week Coach Parcells was telling him how [Redskins offensive lineman] Jeff Bostic was going to eat him up, and it infuriated Jim," said teammate Harry Carson.

So Burt decided on a unique way to both celebrate and get back at his coach after their 17–3 victory over the Redskins. He grabbed the Gatorade cooler, which was still full of the substance, and poured it on Parcells as time expired.

"I was the only one who had the guts to do it without knowing what his reaction was going to be," Burt said.[1]

Burt's teammates were shocked. The first recorded bath was seen almost as a sign of disrespect. The next week, Burt let Carson in on the act. They waited until Parcells took his headphones off, then doused him with the orange-colored drink in the orange cooler.

"You have to remember that we are talking about a ritual, however charming, that's essentially the public demeaning of a football coach, and football coaches are not traditionally tolerant of such behavior," wrote *Washington Post* columnist Tony Kornheiser.[2]

But once it became clear that the Gatorade shower was really a sign of affection that defined the bond between a player and his coach, it became a tradition for the Giants, whose coach actually smiled the first time he was hit with it.

"It's like when you were in school and always used to pick on the chubby guys," Burt told Joan Rivers on her show when asked about the tradition. "That was sort of what we were doing, picking on the chubby guy."[3]

The following season, the stunt caught on nationally in a serendipitous marketing coup that was too good to be true for those who worked on the Gatorade brand.

The Giants lost their season opener to the Cowboys 31–28. The next week, New York beat San Diego 20–7, and at the end of the game Parcells was once again left soaking wet, although Burt was no longer part of the equation. He thought the act had lost its originality. But Carson took it upon himself to keep it going.

"Coach Parcells was very superstitious," Carson said. "If we did something one week and it worked, we did it again. So I kept the Gatorade showers coming, and by the end I think he started to look forward to it."

Parcells didn't mind the showers at all.

"It's fun," Parcells said. "If you have fun, fine. It's not all life and death."[4]

After each victory, Parcells welcomed the baths. Most of the time, the television cameras would focus on Carson and Parcells in the waning minutes of the game, so that viewers wouldn't miss the moment they had come to expect.

The media loved the display. Along with television commentators mentioning it, newspaper writers filled their columns with mentions, even noting the time left in the game when the dunk occurred. The required photo along with each Giants victory was, of course, one of Parcells getting doused.

The Giants finished the regular season 14–2, and even during their week off between the regular season and the playoffs, Gatorade got its exposure. That's because Ahmad Rashad snuck up behind Carson (the guest commentator on CBS's *NFL Today* show) and dumped a Gatorade bucket full of shredded paper on him.

Carson and Parcells Get Paid

Interestingly, Gatorade had no interaction with either Carson or Parcells until the playoffs came.

On January 4, 1987, Bill Schmidt, Gatorade's head of sports marketing at the time, sat down on his couch to watch the Giants play Joe Montana and the San Francisco 49ers. Many people had told him about the Gatorade dunk, but he hadn't caught a glimpse of it yet.

Toward the end of the game, in which the Giants prevailed 49–3 and in the process advanced to the NFC championship game, Carson went to the Gatorade bucket, with the TV cameras following his every move.

"[Announcer] John Madden was circling the Gatorade coolers showing how they do this thing," Schmidt said. "I'm thinking, 'What the hell? I think I've died and gone to heaven.'"

The next day, Schmidt held a meeting to discuss what the brand should do to respond to all the publicity it had received. Schmidt argued that it was best to do nothing, since the company had had nothing to do with it in the first place.

"If a marketer ever tried to create that [Gatorade dunk] moment, it would look fake and phony and contrived," said Tom Fox, currently senior vice president of sports marketing, who worked under Schmidt.

In fact, that had been tried. Burt said that another drink company had called him up after they saw that he was the force behind it all and offered him money to dump its drink on Parcells. He passed.

But now that Schmidt had seen the Gatorade dunk with his own two eyes, he wanted to do something behind the scenes.

"At some point someone was going to ask Coach Parcells if he had heard from Gatorade," Schmidt said.

So Schmidt sent a letter to Carson and Parcells. Enclosed in each was a $1,000 Brooks Brothers gift certificate. (See Appendix B.)

"We at The Quaker Oats Company, makers of Gatorade Thirst Quencher, realize that due to the year-long 'Gatorade dunking' you have been receiving, your wardrobe has probably taken a beating," Schmidt wrote to Parcells. "The enclosed should help remedy the problem; after all, we do feel somewhat responsible for your cleaning bill."

Two days later, Parcells sent a letter back to Schmidt.

"It will be put to good use, and I certainly hope that I'll be getting a few more Gatorade dunkings this year," Parcells wrote.

Despite his anticipation, the next week he begged Carson not to dunk him at the end of the NFC championship game against the Redskins, claiming that it was too cold outside. Carson wouldn't have any of it. Parcells was toast.

The grand stage for the Gatorade bath came two weeks later at Super Bowl XXI in Pasadena, California.

Parcells had been doused with more than 80 gallons of Gatorade during the course of the season, and fans in the stands even had their Gatorade-themed signs, including one that said "Gatorade me," and homemade Gatorade dunk buttons. It was truly a marketer's dream.

The last batch dumped on Parcells was the sweetest. After a 39–20 victory over the Denver Broncos and the 17th and final Gatorade bath of the season, the Giants were crowned champions. The final dunk of the 1986–87 season was named No. 27 on ESPN.com's list of Top 100 Super Bowl moments in 2002.[5]

"When the season was over, the reaction was pretty phenomenal," said Schmidt, whose company made commemorative Gatorade dunk shirts that were sold for $10. "We had corporations in New York who wanted to get their hands on a cooler for their annual meeting so that they could dunk their CEO who had a good year."

Thanks to the national reaction to the Giants, Schmidt decided that he'd take care of Parcells and Carson when the season concluded. He gave Parcells $120,000 over a three-year period and did a $20,000 deal with Carson so that Quaker could include him on a "How to Dunk" poster that was inserted into all the coolers the company sent out.

"It was cheap advertising for Gatorade," Carson said.

The Gatorade bath was now invading all walks of sports and life.

On February 6, 1987, President Ronald Reagan turned 76 years old. As a gift, his staff gave him a cartoon showing an aide pouring a Gatorade bucket on Reagan, who was shouting back, "Really fellas, a simple chorus of 'Happy Birthday' would have been sufficient.'"[6] The following week, when Reagan greeted the Giants, he walked into the Rose Garden with an orange bucket filled with pop-corn and dunked it on Carson.

In March of that same year, after the UNLV Running Rebels had won their 22nd straight basketball game and 37 of the last 38 games to make it to the Final Four, their coach, Jerry Tarkanian, got doused with Gatorade. In September, Minnesota Twins reserve infielder Al Newman took a bucket out of the dugout and poured Gatorade on the pile of players who had just rushed the field to celebrate their American League West title-clinching victory over the Texas Rangers.

The free publicity was great, but the rule at Quaker Oats head-quarters continued to be that the company would never commission a Gatorade bath. The marketers at Quaker knew that if they interfered with the process of celebration, it would have less value.

A short time after the Giants won the Super Bowl, NASCAR marketing executive Bob Weeks called Bill Schmidt. Gatorade had been an official sponsor of NASCAR since 1984. "I'm going to go ahead and get you even better exposure," Weeks said. "I'm going to put the Gatorade logo upside down on the coolers. So when you turn it upside down, the logo will be right side up and people can read it." Schmidt knew that the somewhat spontaneous celebration would die if it were perceived that Gatorade was trying to strain more value out of it, so he told Weeks that he'd rather keep it as it was—the Gatorade logo would be upside down on the dunks. All the dunks would continue to be spontaneous. Agents had called Quaker Oats headquarters saying that their client would dunk a coach after a win if they got paid. No athlete was ever compensated.

That didn't mean that Gatorade wasn't prepared to spend to make sure that there was Gatorade on the sidelines so that the dunks could continue to happen.

The Gatorade Dunk was one of the greatest marketing coups for the brand. Here, New York Giants linebacker Harry Carson dumps head coach Bill Parcells after the Giants win Super Bowl XXI by a score of 39–20. (Getty Images)

"The Gatorade bath meant that people who didn't previously know could see that we were on the sidelines," said Quaker Oats executive Phil Marineau, who oversaw Schmidt's marketing budget. "And I'm thinking, the world is saying, 'We're going to knock these guys off,' or 'We're going to put our name on the cooler,' or 'We're going to make them pay for that—they are not paying for that.' As head of the business at the time, I'm sitting there going, 'God, this is absolutely fantastic, and I've got a budget for this baby.'"

The cooler had started out as a way to allow trainers to mix a large volume of liquid without having to transfer it, but now it was seen as one of the world's first forays into product placement. The success of the Gatorade dunk undoubtedly made the NFL sidelines a more expensive property. This meant that there would be competition.

In 1989, during the week leading up to Super Bowl XXIII, the Cincinnati Bengals and the San Francisco 49ers were practicing in Miami. A few days before the day of the game, a trainer called Bill Schmidt to tell him that the coolers had Diet Coke logos on them. Schmidt soon found out that Diet Coke was the official beverage of the Super Bowl and the sponsor of the halftime show, which it paid for NBC to broadcast in 3-D. Part of the deal included the coolers and Diet Coke logo cups, an inventory that Gatorade helped define. When Schmidt found out about it, he told the NFL that under the terms of their deal, Gatorade had to be on the sidelines. They couldn't put Gatorade in the Diet Coke cups, Schmidt reasoned, because that would constitute something called palming off, a term used to describe a situation in which one brand was representing something manufactured by another brand as its own.

Eventually the league told the trainers that water would go in the Diet Coke cups and Gatorade would go in the Gatorade cups. San Francisco 49ers trainer Lindsy McLean knew that his 49ers drank more water than Gatorade, so he bucked the league's ruling and put the water in the Gatorade cups, so that more Gatorade branding would be apparent to the TV viewers. Perhaps it wasn't coincidence that when the 49ers won, coach Bill Walsh didn't get a Diet Coke bath.

The people controlling Gatorade didn't let something like this happen again. In 1998, Gatorade paid $130 million for six years of sideline rights, more than three times what it had paid for the previous contract. In 2004, Gatorade committed over $500 million to the NFL, including $350 million in rights fees to be spent over the next eight years.

Gatorade officials knew that as long as their product was around the field of play, they'd get exposure they didn't anticipate—like on November 10, 1991. During the halftime show of a game between the San Francisco 49ers and the New Orleans Saints in the Superdome, a rocket from the fireworks show struck a burlap bag used to insulate support wires in the stadium's ceiling. A worker went to put out the fire, but the burning bag fell 200 feet to the field as the third quarter was just getting underway. With the TV cameras rolling and the announcers calling a play-by-play of the fire, a bucket of Gatorade was taken from the sidelines to put the fire out. Gatorade wasn't exactly positioned as a fire extinguisher, but the incident did communicate to the audience that the drink was on the field.

As for the Gatorade bath tradition, it's still very much alive and well. Although Carson finally tired of the Gatorade dunkings, other players did not. (One noticeable change is that many coaches these days are doused with water in the Gatorade bucket, instead of the bright orange liquid that destroyed Parcells's coaching sweaters. Just as there are no contracts that require dunkings, there are no contracts that require that every logoed orange cooler has to have Gatorade in it.)

Best Gatorade Baths

Out of the thousands and thousands of Gatorade baths, a few stand out.

In the most bizarre moment in Gatorade bath history, University of Kentucky head football coach Guy Morriss was left feeling cold and uncomfortable after a premature bath on November 9, 2002.

After Kentucky kicker Taylor Begley hit what appeared to be a game winning 29-yard field goal, the Wildcat players, coaches, and fans were all ready to celebrate their upset victory over the LSU

Tigers. The Wildcats were leading 30–27 with just 13 seconds left, and no one in the stadium expected them to come up short.

The Tigers had the ball at their own 13-yard line, and before their first play of the drive, Kentucky players drenched Morriss with the good ol' Gatorade bath. On the next play, LSU quarterback Marcus Randall threw a 12-yard pass to Michael Clayton. There were two seconds left, and the UK faithful were ready to run onto the field and tear down the goalposts.

Then, on the next and last play of the game, the unthinkable happened. Randall dropped back to pass and launched a prayer. As the ball was in the air, the fireworks on the scoreboard exploded and a sea of blue erupted onto the field at Commonwealth Stadium. The ball came down, and two Wildcat defenders tipped the ball right into the hands of LSU receiver Devery Henderson inside the 20-yard line. He sprinted to the end zone to give the Tigers a 33–30 victory. After the game, Morriss stood cold and wet after what went from a sure win to one of the most astonishing finishes in college football history.

The Wildcats finished the 2002 campaign with a 7–5 record. At the end of the season, Morriss resigned as head coach and took over the head coaching job at Baylor University. In his first win at Baylor, Morriss was given the celebratory bath for the first time since the debacle in Lexington after his team defeated Southern Methodist University 10–7. This time, Morriss's players were smart enough to wait the extra two seconds before Morriss tasted Gatorade once again.

Steve Spurrier might be known as the guy who, as an original guinea pig with the University of Florida football team, helped build the legend of Gatorade. But he also might have been the only coach to retaliate for a Gatorade bath. On November 10, 1990, in his first year as head coach, the team beat Georgia to go to 8–1, Florida's best start since Spurrier's 1966 team began its season with the same record. At the end of the game, Spurrier, seeking revenge on the two Gators defensive linemen who had thrown the Gatorade on him the week before, turned the bucket over on them.

"It was just a glancing blow," a playful Spurrier said afterwards. "I think I startled them a little bit. I guess they didn't know it was legal [to do that]."[7]

The Deadly Dunk

Periodically, doctors have warned players that a Gatorade bath might not be the best thing for the coach. An acupuncturist named Eugene Iwasa has specifically talked about the hazards of such a bath. Iwasa says that there is a danger that cold liquid will hit two acupuncture points on the back and the neck. The cold could inhibit the flow of blood to these areas and lead to neck and back pain, a cold, or even pneumonia. Iwasa jokes that it would be better for people to soak their coaches with warm tea.

Only once has a dunk turned deadly.

Legendary coach George Allen had a tremendous career in the NFL. From 1966 to 1977, he amassed an impressive 116–47–5 record with the Los Angeles Rams and the Washington Redskins. After a brief stint in the USFL in 1983 and 1984, Allen retired from the game for five years before being called back into action to coach the Long Beach State 49ers at the age of 71.

Allen accepted the job because it was only 25 miles from his home in Palos Verdes, and it was certainly the most challenging job he could possibly take. Not only had the team had only one winning season in its last six, it was hemorrhaging financially—it averaged only 2,650 fans per home game in the season prior to Allen's arrival—

and it frequently played UCLA, USC, and Michigan on the road in exchange for cash.

After opening the season with three losses, Allen's 49ers won five of the next seven, and on November 17, 1990, they faced the UNLV Running Rebels for a chance to finish the season with a 6–5 record.

Ahead 29–20 with 45 seconds to go, the Long Beach State players looked around at each other. They knew it was time to celebrate. Two players made their way to the Gatorade, conveniently located directly behind the 49ers bench. They picked up a Gatorade bucket, tiptoed toward Allen, and dumped it on him.

Six weeks later, Allen passed away from what was ruled to be heart failure. But in an interview shortly before his death, he said that he hadn't been healthy ever since he got the bath.

"They dumped a bucket of Gatorade on me, only it wasn't Gatorade, because we can't afford Gatorade," Allen said. "It was ice water."[8]

Every once in a while, as a sign of respect, an expected Gatorade bath does not take place. On November 14, 1993, when Miami Dolphins coach Don Shula became the winningest coach in NFL history, the coolers stayed on the ground.

"They didn't want him looking like a drowned rat. They wanted him looking like a king," wrote Bill Plaschke of the *Los Angeles Times*. "A classy man," guard Keith Sims said. "We looked at the Gatorade and said, 'You know, we need to do a classy thing.'"[9]

Instead, the Dolphins carried Shula off the field.

Holding the bucket actually became the subject of an ad campaign launched by one of Gatorade's competitors in 1991. In this spot, not coincidentally filmed at Giants Stadium, a football team hesitates to dump a cooler full of Pepsi's sports drink Mountain Dew

Sport on its coach. The voice-over says, "Tastes so good, you won't want to spill a drop."

Parcells and Carson will always be associated with Gatorade. Carson had a 13-year career that included nine Pro Bowls, but today, the photograph he is most commonly asked to autograph at card shows is that of him throwing Gatorade on Parcells.

Carson often gets the credit for the Gatorade dunk, even though Jim Burt was the actual inventor—or so we thought until 1999, when Chicago Bears Hall of Fame defensive lineman Dan Hampton claimed that he actually executed the first dunk. This prompted a reporter for the *Daily Herald* in Chicago to review a video of the game between the Bears and the Minnesota Vikings in week 13 of the 1984 season. With time still on the clock but the Bears safely assured of clinching the NFC Central Division title, Steve McMichael was holding Bears coach Mike Ditka while Hampton and fellow teammate Mike Singletary moved in.

"I stood in front of him as the game was still going on, and he was protesting, 'Get away from me,'" McMichael wrote in his recently published book. "He couldn't figure out why I was talking to him when he was trying to run a game. I actually had to grab his shoulders and hold him, and Dan came from behind and just doused him. That's when the Gatorade baths started."[10]

Perhaps Hampton's mistake was that he and his teammates didn't perform the act again when the Bears thrashed the New England Patriots in Super Bowl XX in 1986.

"What were we going to say?" Hampton said. "We should have been back there in 1986 winning our second straight Super Bowl. Were we going to whine about the Gatorade thing?"[11]

No matter who invented the dunk, it is arguable that no brand has ever received more free publicity than Gatorade got and is still getting from the dunk.

"There are things that happen serendipitously, but for the most part you create your own luck," said former Gatorade executive Peter Vitulli. "If you depend on it, you will be disappointed. But many brands create opportunities and good things just happen—like having the product on the sidelines allowed Harry Carson to dump it on Bill Parcells. Years earlier, having it on the sidelines allowed the Georgia Tech coach [Bobby Dodd] to say that Gatorade made the difference in Florida's winning the game."

Said Schmidt: "The Gatorade dunk basically meant we had arrived. Mainstream America included mom, apple pie, Chevrolet, and now Gatorade."

In 2004, video game maker Electronic Arts (whose motto is "If it's in the game, it's in the game") brought out a new version of its most popular sports franchise, Madden NFL 2005. For the first time in the game's 16-year history, gamers could douse their coaches with Gatorade after a big victory.

Also in 2004, Glaceau Vitamin Water, which has positioned itself as the anti-sport drink, put Gatorade dunk references on its bottle:

> It has come to our attention that, at the conclusion of some sporting events, athletes pour large buckets of a "sports drink" over their coach's head. Not to be outdone, we encourage our loyal consumers to do the same after a grueling match. O.K., sure. Dumping this over your chess team coach's head may sound strange, but trust us, nothing gets chess fans more pumped up.

Following the Giants' dunkings, Gatorade officials steadily improved the use of the sidelines for product placement. They changed the color of the waxed paper cup to make it brighter and easier to see.

Thanks to listening to the trainers' needs, they provided free squeeze bottles (with the Gatorade logo on them, of course) and towels, which were of a higher quality than the towels that many of the teams had—the price paid was the smattering of Gatorade logos on them.

Eventually, Gatorade officials devised a prearranged package that went out to football, basketball, and baseball teams at the start of every training season. Each team would get coolers, towels, and a logoed holder that would allow football assistants to easily carry six squeeze bottles to the players. Extra supplies were then stocked in a fully staffed 60,000-square-foot warehouse, where employees would make sure that every trainer had the number of Gatorade coolers, cups, and towels that he or she needed.

Gatorade became so good at doing this and established such a presence that a very select group of companies saw the value of creating similar branding inventories.

When Wendy's put its logo on cups in the early 1980s to replace Gatorade's presence on the Miami Dolphins sidelines, it didn't make sense. When Charles Schwab logos appeared on coolers, squeeze bottles, and cups for the Bowl Championship Series games in 1999, it looked absurd. The financial services company didn't do it again.

In February 2005, the television broadcast of Super Bowl XXXIX showed the Gatorade logo on cups, towels, and coolers for a total of 6 minutes and 58 seconds. With all the fans watching the game around the world, Gatorade received more than 590 million impressions, according to Nielsen's Sports Sponsorship Scorecard.

Said Gatorade's current head of sports marketing, Tom Fox: "If you look today at what people are trying to do as they think about

TiVo in the future, and as companies are trying to find a way to link themselves with sports in a really meaningful way, you keep coming back to the fact that those products (Gatorade coolers and cups) have been there for more than 30 years in a way that the consumer has grown to expect."

CHAPTER 6

"Be Like Mike"

IN THE FALL of 1990, executives from Quaker and Gatorade flew to Italy for marketing meetings with their European counterparts. In a hotel boardroom were Peter Vitulli, by now U.S. president of Quaker specialty foods; Gatorade's sports marketing head Bill Schmidt; Quaker marketers Peggy Dyer and Matt Mannelly; and Giulio Malgara, who was president of Quaker's European businesses.

Although the American and European teams were marketing the same beverage, this much was clear: They had two divergent marketing plans. In America, ad spending was focused more on the message than on the athletes. League associations provided Gatorade moments on live broadcasts with professional athletes in genuine situations. This served as the confirmation that the best of the world's athletes at least used the product.

Malgara ran his own ship in Italy, where Gatorade had been launched in 1987 and had successfully emerged as the No. 1 sports drink. By all accounts, he liked being around athletes. He liked the fact the brand that he was in charge of was splashed over the sports that he loved. He wanted to rub elbows with everybody, and that often meant doing deals that didn't fall in line with the overall strategy of the business.

At the time of the meeting, more than 20 individual European athletes were paid endorsers of Gatorade. Malgara even put Gatorade money behind a boat in the Whitbread Round the World Race, a competition in which contestants vied for first place in the 32,000-mile journey.

"I asked him one time, 'How many people are in the stands to watch the boat sail around the world?'" Schmidt said.

Malgara's tactics wouldn't have been tolerated at Quaker's headquarters in the United States, where the marketing team's rule of thumb was never to call attention to Gatorade in an unnatural way. In Europe, Malgara was paying cameramen shooting soccer games to get the best shots of the Gatorade coolers in the background. All told, his annual marketing budget was north of $25 million—more than the budget of his American counterparts, who were dealing with a business that was at least five times the size.

But Giulio Malgara also had a purpose at this meeting in Milan. He didn't understand why those who were managing Gatorade's brand on the other side of the Atlantic were so scared of paying a professional athlete for an endorsement. It wasn't that they thought that it wouldn't work. The first issue was that early Quaker focus groups indicated that the public thought athlete endorsers were borrowed interests, and they didn't necessarily believe that the athlete would actually use the product if he or she weren't being paid to do so.

"What is more credible than when you see a guy hit a basket, score a touchdown, or hit a grand slam home run, then walk to the bench and slug down a Gatorade?" Quaker Oats executive Phil Marineau said. "That says it's the real deal."

During the first seven years of Quaker's ownership, not one professional athlete was featured in national advertising. That fact was extremely ironic given that Quaker was one of the first companies to use celebrity testimonials. In 1934, the same year that Wheaties put Lou Gehrig and Jimmy Foxx on its first boxes, Quaker used New York Yankees slugger Babe Ruth to advertise the company's Puffed Wheat and Puffed Rice.

But without using athlete endorsements, the brand had grown rapidly thanks to broadened availability and a targeted campaign that was meant to acquaint potential active consumers with the benefits of the drink.

The Thirst Aid Campaign

Soon after the acquisition of Stokely came the advertising debut of "Demo-man," a computer-generated image that showed the inside of a person's body as he drank Gatorade. As the solution went down into the body and rehydration occurred, the colors changed.

When Gatorade executives became more confident that their ads were educating consumers, "Demo-man" became less the focus and the spirit of Gatorade took over. More and more spots showed people in what Quaker executives referred to as "Gatorade moments"—drinking Gatorade during a break or after their recreational league basketball or soccer game.

From 1984 to 1990, the television advertising came complete with a jingle that said it all: "Gatorade is thirst aid, for that deep down body thirst!" The jingle was very popular and proved to be extremely effective.

In fact, the jingle was so effective that according to a survey done in 1987 by a veteran advertising researcher, 79.2 percent of consumers filled in the phrase "_____ is thirst aid" with the word "Gatorade."

"The only slogan recognized by more consumers was 'This _____ for you' (Answer: Bud's). The Thirst Aid slogan was recognized by more consumers than 'Fly the friendly skies of _____' (Answer: United)."[1]

The slogan said everything that executives wanted to convey to consumers, and it worked. Sales continued to rise under the Thirst Aid campaign. From July 1984 to June 1985, Gatorade netted $171 million. Sales went up by at least 25 percent each year, so that by the end of 1990, sales were approaching $900 million annually.[2] But in December of 1990, Quaker officials were told by the courts to cease using "Thirst Aid." Throughout the entire life of the campaign, the use of the slogan "Thirst Aid" had been challenged by Sands, Taylor & Woods, a company that held this trademark for use on over a hundred products relating to fountain and beverage syrups and ice cream toppings.

Quaker officials thought that the company's use of "Thirst Aid" was fair use and didn't conflict with the trademark holders. But Sands, Taylor & Woods argued that Gatorade's advertising was so effective that it rendered the mark, which it was intent on licensing to other companies, useless. Gatorade, by association, had made the mark its own. Sands, Taylor & Woods was eventually awarded $16.3 million, one of the largest awards in trademark infringement history.

With the "Thirst Aid" campaign ending, it was possible that a step in a new direction would also signal the company's willingness to conform to what had now become the standard sports endorsement model.

By 1990, sports marketing was quickly changing. Led by the success that Nike had had with Chicago Bulls guard Michael Jordan, companies were using professional athletes to help sell their products more than ever before. The thinking was that if you were a fan of a particular athlete, you might be more likely to buy a product if that athlete told you to or if his face was plastered on the packaging. In the marketing world, the transposition of emotion from an athlete or sporting event to a particular brand was referred to as the "halo effect."

It wasn't happening just in the sneaker industry. Jordan himself had a deal with Coca-Cola. Los Angeles Lakers guard Magic Johnson pitched Pepsi, and Miami Dolphins quarterback Dan Marino, San Francisco 49ers quarterback Joe Montana, and dual-sport athlete Bo Jackson shilled for Diet Pepsi.

Looking for a new direction, the Gatorade marketers found themselves in Italy, with Malgara challenging them to use professional athletes in their next big campaign.

Schmidt wanted only one athlete: Michael Jordan.

Wooing Michael Jordan

Jordan was perfect for a company like Quaker Oats. The company was based in Chicago, and he was the city's biggest star. Jordan had been in the league for seven seasons and had led the league in scoring for the past five years. In the 1990–91 season, the Chicago Bulls won their first championship by beating the Los Angeles Lakers with Magic Johnson. At the age of 27, Jordan had already won the league MVP award twice.

From the start, Jordan actually had a stronger connection with Gatorade than he did with Nike. Before he signed with Nike in 1984, Jordan had worn only Adidas and Converse sneakers. But he had been a Gatorade drinker when he was growing up. In early conversations with Gatorade officials, he told them that he had had a stash of it in his garage when he played for Laney High School in Wilmington, North Carolina. Jordan continued to drink Gatorade at North Carolina, where as a freshman in the 1982 NCAA championship game against Patrick Ewing and the Georgetown Hoyas, he hit the game-winning shot.

When he reached the NBA, Jordan would lose as much as five pounds in water weight per game. His personal trainer, Tim Grover, had called the Gatorade Sports Science Institute for a solution. The result? One bottle of Gatorade 45 minutes before the game, one or two bottles during the game, and one bottle afterwards.

"He loves the stuff," Grover said.[3]

When he built the workout facility in his house, he made sure there was a fridge nearby—stacked top to bottom with Gatorade, of course.

Gatorade was also there when Jordan had one of his most memorable performances, one that shaped his legacy. In February 1988, the All-Star Game was played in Chicago Stadium, and Gatorade sponsored the Slam Dunk Contest. In the semifinals of the event, Jordan dribbled the length of the court, took off at the foul line, did a double clutch, and slammed it down.

The famous picture of this event, which has been blown up to every size imaginable by his fans, features "His Airness" from the ground, looking up at him as he approaches the rim on the free-throw dunk. Clearly visible on the scoreboard is "Gatorade Thirst Quencher," and there is a ball rack with the Gatorade logo on it in the far background. (This wasn't by accident. Schmidt had scouted out the arena beforehand and knew where the best points of exposure would be.)

In 1985, Quaker had actually made an unsuccessful pitch for Jordan's services. At the time, Gatorade was paying the NFL only about $100,000 for its rights, so it surely couldn't budget $300,000 per year in marketing to give to Jordan. So Jordan's agent, David Falk, came up with the cross-platform pitch: Jordan would endorse Gatorade, a cereal, and granola bars.

"I wanted to do Life Cereal because of those famous commercials where they say, 'Mikey Likes It,'" Falk said. But the only major interest in Jordan's services within Quaker was from Diane Primo, who was in charge of marketing for Quaker's Beanie Weenies brand (beans and hot dogs in a sauce).

"He actually ate Beanie Weenies as a kid," Falk said. "But I thought that if I called Michael up and told him I got him a deal to endorse Gatorade and Beanie Weenies, he'd fire me."

When Quaker was unable to come up with the money, Jordan went to Coca-Cola, a product that he had also been drinking since his early childhood. Six years after the first discussion with Quaker, Jordan—thanks to his on-the-court wizardry and off-the-court charisma—was deemed the ultimate pitchman by many. During the 1990–91 season, he earned $2.5 million for his work on the court, but he earned about $10 million off it, more than the payroll of some NBA teams.

He was the face of Nike, which had made six signature Air Jordan shoes since signing him as a rookie. Commercials with Spike Lee as Mars Blackmon (the best player on Mars) and Jordan (the best player on Earth) received national acclaim. Besides Nike and Coca-Cola, Jordan also had deals with McDonald's, General Mills (to endorse Wheaties), Sara Lee (to pitch Hanes underwear), and Wilson (for his own signature line of basketballs). His image was plastered on clothing and trinkets. There were Michael Jordan valentines by Cleo, Michael Jordan gift wrap, and, yes, even Michael Jordan "Hangtime" gum.

Jordan was so big that the Bulls coming into town probably meant the closest form of hero worship since the Beatles. When he stepped up to the foul line, hundreds of flashes went off from the cameras in the stands. For the people taking the pictures, it was their chance to get perhaps a once-in-a-lifetime picture of Jordan.

Gatorade officials wanted to have a stake in that experience. And by 1990, the brand had a budget that might possibly be able to meet Jordan's asking price.

Jordan Signs $13.5 Million Deal

While Vitulli, Dyer, Mannelly, and Malgara were conversing, Schmidt left the meeting to call Falk. Falk told Schmidt that Jordan's second Coke contract would expire in July, and that he would be interested in having Gatorade in the negotiations. Schmidt was shocked. Contracts like these normally gave the incumbent the right of first refusal.

From Gatorade's standpoint, it helped that Coca-Cola really wasn't particularly getting much bang for its buck from Jordan. He was used infrequently in the company's advertising, and his appearances weren't particularly memorable. In one spot, three kids in a tree house argue about who is supposed to bring them their Coca-Cola Classic. Moments after they yell, "Michael," Jordan—holding a six-pack of Coke—leaps into the air and delivers the soda to the tree house. Another spot had Jordan defying gravity, jumping past the moon to reach a Coca-Cola bottle floating in space.

The truth was that, at the time, the soft drink advertising business was more focused on entertainers than on sports endorsers. Jordan was just one of many options for the company, along with the New Kids on the Block, Aretha Franklin, Paula Abdul, and Elton John.

In February 1991, Schmidt and Falk met in Charlotte, North Carolina, the location of the NBA All-Star Game that year. At a bar, the two started throwing out numbers. Schmidt said that he would be willing to commit to Jordan for five years. But Falk had just finished reading a story on Jack Nicklaus's marketing deals, most of which were 10-year deals. He knew that his client was reaching iconic status like the Golden Bear. When Schmidt left Falk that night, he was well aware of what it would take to get Jordan.

Written on a cocktail napkin was, "10 years, seven figures per year." Falk was prepared for a bidding war. His sources told him that Whitney Houston was making $1.8 million and Elton John was being paid more than $2 million by Coke. He thought his client was on that superstar level, and he knew that Coke had more cash than Quaker's Gatorade brand. In a move that might have helped seal the deal for Gatorade, Jordan prohibited Falk from going back and forth.

"Michael always had a desire to know what people thought he was worth, as opposed to what I was capable of getting for him," Falk said. "And so he wanted to know without a bidding contest."

Falk had already told Schmidt what he expected, so he felt it was only fair to give Chuck Morrison, the head of ethnic marketing for Coca-Cola, the same parameters—10 years, seven figures per year. Jordan had just turned 28. It wasn't likely that he would be in the league for 10 more years. The contract would not include a right to terminate if Jordan walked off the basketball court. But that was the price to pay, the risk, for companies that wanted to continue or forge new relationships with Jordan, whose NBA championship the year before, 1991, made him complete.

Coca-Cola crumbled under the pressure. It offered a five-year deal at $750,000 per year. Gatorade stepped up to the table, satisfying Falk's wishes with a ten-year deal worth $13.5 million. Jordan would be paid $1 million a year for seven years, $2 million a year for two years, and $2.5 million for another year. An added bonus in the deal was that Schmidt had promised that Jordan would be the exclusive spokesperson for the brand.

"It was the Secretariat strategy," said Quaker marketer Matt Mannelly, whose brother Pat was devastated to learn of the switch, since he was the chief financial officer at Coca-Cola at the time. "While Coke was going to have a different person all the time, we'd say that we would have only one horse."

Not only did Gatorade have Jordan, but it prevented Coca-Cola from using him for its upstart sports drink POWERade, which was introduced in 1990.

"I think if you had kept Michael with Coca-Cola and the advertising was well done, they would have been able to dramatically penetrate Gatorade's dominance in the marketplace," Falk said.

Falk certainly wasn't complaining. The 10-year deal that Gatorade had agreed to became the model for every company looking for a relationship with Jordan. From then on, Falk insisted that if a company wanted to borrow the tremendous equity that Jordan had in the endorsement world, it had to sign a 10-year deal. Companies like Sara Lee and WorldCom signed on, while others (including McDonald's) decided to go in a different direction. The Gatorade deal was completed in principle in the late spring, but Jordan's contract with

Coca-Cola didn't expire until July. In the meantime, Gatorade officials scrambled to make sure that they were ready to unveil a commercial as soon as their contract with Jordan could legally commence.

There was a lot of hesitation at first. Hank Steinbrecher, who had worked on the Gatorade brand from 1985 to 1990 and had recently left the company, called Schmidt when he heard that the company was going to announce a deal with Jordan. He told his former boss that he thought the deal was a mistake.

"I was thinking, 'God, we were growing the brand based on having a preeminence on the field and on the court, and now they're going to go the individual athlete route?'" Steinbrecher said.

He wasn't the only one who was unsure about the strategy.

"Signing this massive professional athlete and for such a sizable amount of money was kind of like, 'Wait a minute, what are we doing?'" said longtime Gatorade executive Cindy Alston. "I think a lot of people were saying, 'We love Michael Jordan at a Chicago-based company,' but there was a lot of angst about getting it right."

"Gatorade had always stood for being for team, win or lose," Dyer said. "Not for an individual star athlete. And that [signing Michael] challenged some of the core values of the brand in terms of what we stand for and does this mean that we support only people who are star athletes, only those who are winners. But we thought Michael was just so extraordinary and so exceptional that he could transcend all of that."

"Be Like Mike"

Knowing that this was a big moment, Gatorade's advertising firm at the time, Bayer Bess Vanderwarker, brought back its creative chief, Bernie Pitzel, who had moved to another Chicago advertising firm.

He was lured back by the fact that he was going to introduce Jordan and Gatorade to the world.

But when he arrived, he found out that the first commercials had already been approved. One played off the true story of a kid in Yugoslavia who wrote a letter addressed to "Michael Jordan. USA," and it actually arrived in the hands of Gatorade's spokesperson. Another showed highlights of Jordan dominating opponents and doing his signature dunks. The latter spot had already been approved by all the top executives at Quaker.

"I was totally stunned," Pitzel said. "It was just a highlight reel—a video of him dunking—and Nike had done that over and over again. I was thinking, 'I came over here to do this and this is what we did?'"

Pitzel was given three days to come up with something different, although there were no guarantees that it would beat out the spot that was planned—the one that he had so despised. That night, he went home frustrated that he couldn't think of anything. He sat down to watch a movie with his younger son. Disney had recently re-released its 1967 classic animated film *The Jungle Book*. When he heard "I Wan'na Be Like You," the Monkey Song in the film, it immediately clicked.

"I knew that a million people wanted to be like Mike," Pitzel said.

It was hard to ignore. Number 23 was quickly becoming the most popular jersey among high school and college players. Pitzel had planned to run *The Jungle Book* music over the video, with a final screen saying, "Be Like Mike. Drink Gatorade." But that plan was quickly undone when he found out that Disney officials wanted $350,000 to allow Gatorade to use the song for a five-week commercial run. Plan B was to develop his own lyric, mimicking the sentiments of the idol worship of Jordan, but not infringing on the lyrics owned by Disney.

So Pitzel went to his favorite restaurant, Avanzare (where he did all his creative work), sat down at a table with pen in hand, and started writing the lyrics to "Be Like Mike" on the paper tablecloth:

Sometimes I dream
That he is me
You've got to see that's how I dream to be
I dream I move, I dream I groove
Like Mike
If I could Be Like Mike
Again I try
Just need to fly
For just one day if I could
Be that way
I dream I move
I dream I groove
Like Mike
If I could Be Like Mike[4]

Four hours later, he was faxing a ripped tablecloth with the lyrics to four different local music companies, hoping that one of them would come up with a catchy tune. Everything, Pitzel said, had to be done in 48 hours.

Ira Antelis and his business partner, Steve Shafer, a local pair of jingle writers, had a chance at the poem.

"I figured I would make more of a song out of it, take the 'Be Like Mike' and really make it the chorus," said Antelis, who was intrigued by the opportunity thanks to his love for the NBA. Antelis hired eight singers to sing the work, and when he was done, he knew that it was a smash and that no other company would beat it. He was right.

That day, with no sleep, Pitzel and Tony Vanderwarker drove the tape of Antelis and Shafer's creation to the American Club in Kohler, Wisconsin, where Gatorade executives were meeting. There, they heard "Be Like Mike" for the first time, from a tape played on a boom box. No words had to be spoken. They knew that they had a winner.

There was initial skepticism about the phrase "Be Like Mike." The fact was that Jordan really wasn't ever called Mike in the public spotlight. Gatorade and Quaker Oats executives worried that Jordan would mind and that it would get the relationship off to a bad start. Falk wasn't initially thrilled, but Jordan had no issues with it.

"The dunking made him a god, and what we were trying to do was humanize him and bring him down to a level to make him more acceptable," Pitzel said. "As long as he allowed us to do it, which he did, it was going to work."

Pitzel then dreamed up the commercial's image. He commissioned a group of kids—including many children of Quaker executives—to try to be like Jordan in front of Jordan at a basketball court in Chicago. He also got shots of Jordan goofing around and drinking the product.

To Pitzel's credit, the spot didn't feature great basketball players. It featured kids who weren't stellar at all, but merely dreamed of being like Jordan. In fact, Pitzel's 13-year-old son Nathan is one of the stars of the commercial. He tries to dribble the ball through his legs, but things don't exactly work out.

On August 8, 1991, Quaker officials, 2,000 strong, gathered outside the Quaker Tower to see the announcement of their prize brand's new spokesman. Tubs of Gatorade littered the tent over the parking lot, and the spot—which ended with "Be Like Mike. Drink Gatorade"—was shown to the crowd.

In Gatorade's 26-year history, this was definitely its shining moment. It was arguably Quaker Oats's shining moment as well. After all, only a few months before, Gatorade had, for the first time, passed oatmeal in sales.

One media member, predictably, asked Jordan when he had changed his name to Mike.

"You can call me Mike, Michael or Air. I'll get used to it,"[5] Jordan replied.

Within hours, "Be Like Mike" was on television. Quaker officials paid $1 million to run an eight-page ad that turned into a poster of Jordan posing in the same way he did for Nike's "Wings" poster, this time with that familiar waxed Gatorade cup in his hand.

"After leading the league in scoring," the ad began. "After taking the Bulls to the Eastern Conference Championship. And after winning the NBA title, what is there left to reach for?" When the reader turned the page, the green cup was revealed. Quaker officials weren't intending to copy the Nike black-and-white poster, but Nike still threatened to sue. Nothing materialized.

The next week, "Be Like Mike" was running in movie theatres.

"I say that when we signed Michael, Michael was bigger than the brand," said Tom Fox, who began his work with Quaker in 1985. "I think we knew that we had a product that worked, and we saw we were on the cusp, from a marketing perspective, of becoming a product that was more mainstream. That instead of people looking at us as 'Oh, that's what serious athletes drink,' we thought we could create that linkage with, 'Hey, I'm hot, I'm sweaty, that's what I should be drinking.'"

The advertisement was a huge hit, but Quaker Oats took it a step further. The company made cassettes of four versions of "Be Like Mike" and passed them out to radio stations. Three months after the commercial was first aired, approximately 100,000 copies were available to the public for $4.95 each, with proceeds going to the Michael Jordan Foundation.

Opposing NBA teams got their hands on the cassette, and the song was used when the Bulls came to town, not shying away from the fact that the arena was often sold out because of the visitor. For Gatorade, it was free commercial after free commercial.

"If we had used the music from *The Jungle Book*, the advertisement would have been forgotten," Antelis said. "Instead, we generated a piece of music that we could own that the world could identify with Gatorade."

Anchors on ESPN's *SportsCenter* all of a sudden started to occasionally refer to Jordan as "Mike," a moment that executive Matt Mannelly says was evidence that "we had hit a home run."

"When we signed Jordan, beyond the court he was pretty much 100 percent associated with Nike," Mannelly said. "But after 'Be Like Mike,' Gatorade was all of a sudden part of the equation."

Perhaps greater evidence of the power of the spot could be found on the streets of America, where kids across the nation almost immediately echoed the sentiments of the commercial; they too wanted to "Be Like Mike."

"I had a kid at a Cubs game wanting my autograph because he was singing it behind me and my kids told him that I had written it," Pitzel said. "It became part of pop culture, and as an ad guy, that's basically what you are trying to do with everything."

The spot was not without its critics, some of whom panned the implicit promise of becoming like the greatest athlete of all time by drinking the magic Gatorade potion.

"Take a tip from the advertising world: If you talk to the hearts and needs of listeners, their minds and dollar bills will follow," wrote

Chicago Bulls star Michael Jordan signed a 10-year, $13.5 million deal to endorse Gatorade in 1991. Jordan's contract was extended until 2007. (Walter Iooss Jr./NBAE/Getty Images)

two columnists from the *Atlanta Journal-Constitution*. "Gatorade's goal in this spot is to sell to young people. They do not say, 'Buy Gatorade. It will regenerate your electrolytes.' That holds no interest to the teen market. 'Be like Mike' is the incentive."[6]

"The 'dream' reference in the lyric, suggesting unattainable fantasy, presumably is designed to deflect criticism about over-selling Gatorade's efficacy," wrote Bob Garfield in *Advertising Age*. "But the distinction will be lost on all 10-year-olds and most adults, who are being led to an enticing and false conclusion about this 'sports drink': the promise of Michael-esque performance."[7]

Gatorade, of course, wasn't alone in using this premise; Nike had been using the same sales tactic for years with Air Jordans. And it worked.

The best account of this sheer idol worship and its connection to the endorser's product can be found in Bob Greene's book, *Hang Time: Days and Dreams with Michael Jordan.*

It was October 26, 1991, and "Be Like Mike" had been out for almost three months when the Chicago Bulls played a meaningless exhibition game against the Denver Nuggets in front of a crowd of 31,278 people at the Louisiana Superdome. The number of fans in attendance was particularly impressive given that 80 miles away, the LSU football team was playing the Florida State Seminoles, who were ranked number one in the country at the time.

Following a 135–108 rout by the Bulls, Jordan and the others made their way to the team bus. A group of fans followed Jordan and his entourage for an autograph, or perhaps just a closer glimpse. The scene that Greene described not only told of the power of Jordan's appeal, but also told of the success of Gatorade's marketing of him. As Greene wrote,

> Just before he got to the bus, his path took him close to two very little children, really tiny, probably no more than four years old. The boys were dressed in scruffy, raggedy clothes, and there was no adult visible who appeared to be supervising them; it was puzzling that they would be here so late at night. They said nothing until Jordan was within a few feet of them, and then as if they had planned.
>
> "I want to Be Like Mike," one of the boys called, with no smile on his face and a desperate tenor to his voice. "I want to be like you, Mike," the other boy called.
>
> The commercial had only been on the air for a few weeks by now, but it had reached these boys in Louisiana. The police

officers hurried forward. "I want to be like you Mike," one of the boys called again, almost crying. "I want to be like Mike," his companion shouted in the smallest of voices over and over and over, not taking a breath. It was as if the boys believed that, were they to catch sight of Jordan and recite the magic words, something good might happen to them.

The police hustled Jordan further along, towards the bus, and the boys, by necessity, shortened their phrases. "Be Like Mike," they called to him. "Be Like Mike." It was a plea.[8]

It's not known whether those young kids were Gatorade drinkers, but the odds are that they knew about the product because of the advertising, which in 2004 was named by ESPN as the seventh best sports commercial in the last 25 years.

"It wasn't the greatest tasting beverage, but if kids wanted to 'Be Like Mike,' they knew they had to drink it," said Michael Bellas, chairman and CEO of the Beverage Marketing Corporation.

For Quaker, it wasn't enough to have a Jordan fan try a Gatorade; the company wanted that fan to become a loyal consumer. In order for that to happen, the fans would have to either grow to like Gatorade or perceive that it somehow worked for them.

This was one of the reasons why, in 1992, the "Be Like Mike" song stayed on, but the images changed to Jordan on the court.

"The original advertising wasn't as effective as we had hoped," Dyer said. "It was to have broad market appeal, and what we needed to do, we learned, was to be effective to the brand's target. When we brought it back to real highlights with Michael sweating, it worked better."

In his first three years with the brand, Jordan was featured in an unbelievable 14 commercials. The relationship was going along great. In 1992, Gatorade made life-size Michael Jordan cutouts that it sent to retailers in order to try to command some space. This helped get the new 16-ounce bottles into stores. But Jordan was so popular that most of the cutouts never reached the store floors. Vendors pocketed some of them for their own use; others were soon being sold at sports collectibles shops. Gatorade executives didn't care that much—they were pleased that they had created something that was becoming a hard-to-find item.

"Gatorade was the sort of product that had a funny taste and a funny green color that came in a big glass bottle—this [signing Jordan] put us on the map as a mainstream consumer brand," Fox said. "Nobody was more popular than Michael Jordan. Nobody signified performance at a higher level."

Not only was Jordan dominating on the court, he was superb off of it. And Schmidt did more than any marketer with whom Jordan had a relationship to make sure that when it came time for Jordan to perform at a shoot, he gave his A performance. At each commercial shoot, Jordan knew that he'd have a box of Montecristo No. 2 Cuban torpedo cigars waiting for him. Schmidt, with his boss Phil Marineau's approval, made sure that Quaker Oats accounting knew that this expense was coming every time. The $500 cost for the box of 25 was seen as a necessary expense.

"I knew how to manage him," Schmidt said. "I knew who he wanted at the shoot and who he didn't want. Other people would hire the caterer that they liked most. I hired the one that he liked most—that made his favorite chili."

Schmidt had worked on every detail. The security guards at the shoot were the same guards that he was accustomed to seeing at the arena. When Jordan was called for four hours, it never went over.

To assure that, Schmidt had a body double come to each shoot beforehand to block out the scene.

"No one did a better job, in any company, of managing the relationship with Michael," Falk said. "Bill protected Michael from crazy requests that would come through the company. 'Can Michael do this? Can Michael do that?' Most of that stuff, probably 90 percent, I never heard about."

Jordan was such an icon on the court that off-the-court news somehow didn't damage his business relationships. In 1992 and 1993, Jordan's gambling habit became news. He admitted to losing $57,000 in bets to a man who turned out to be a drug dealer, and a year later a San Diego businessman named Richard Esquinas claimed that he had won $1.25 million from Jordan by beating Jordan in rounds of golf over a 10-day period. Jordan acknowledged that they had played, but said that he had lost less than what Esquinas claimed.

This was the risk in signing an individual athlete that so many in the company had worried about, and it appeared that even Jordan, who was perceived as squeaky clean, could be corruptible.

"It's hard to believe that the sports drink marketer really wants to continue its 'Be like Mike' theme, not when fans are holding up placards with that slogan and a pair of dice underneath,"[9] said an editorial in *Advertising Age*.

In the end, Jordan's actions never tarnished the Gatorade brand, and the alliance between the two prospered with very few bumps in the road—until October 4, 1993, that is.

His Airness Retires

On that day, Quaker Oats chairman Bill Smithburg took Bill Schmidt as his guest to play two rounds of golf with Michael Jordan and Fred Couples. Smithburg had paid $20,000 for the foursome in a Jordan Foundation auction, and he figured he would take his business partner along for the ride.

After play was finished that day at the Windsor Club in Vero Beach, Florida, the four went to the Monday Night Football game (the Washington Redskins at the Miami Dolphins) that night. In the luxury suite, Jordan was ahead of Schmidt on the buffet line. After grabbing a piece of chicken, he turned around and tapped Schmidt—who was facing in the other direction—on the shoulder.

"Hey Billy," Jordan said. "I'm going to announce my retirement on Wednesday. But you can't tell anyone."

Schmidt, who had received a Bulls championship ring from the team's third title as a gift from Jordan, was obviously extremely uncomfortable with the decision from a business standpoint, but he hugged Jordan and told him he was happy for him. He had known that this day could come at any minute. Jordan had already won three championships.

Two days later, Jordan made the news official, saying that he had nothing left to prove in the sport he so dominated. The news immediately derailed Gatorade's plans.

A new advertisement that had Jordan playing in his Bulls uniform in Chicago Stadium was in the can. It had to be pulled. Two months later, it was clear that Jordan was going to try his hand at baseball. On February 7, 1994, he signed a minor league contract with the Chicago White Sox, and soon after he was assigned to play Double-A ball with the Birmingham Barons. Jordan batted .202 with 51 RBIs and struck out 114 times in 127 games. A *Sports Illustrated* cover showed a picture of Jordan swinging and missing with a screaming headline, "Bag It, Michael!" Jordan didn't speak to *Sports Illustrated* reporters too much after that.

Gatorade featured Jordan in a few baseball spots, including one that showed him as a pitcher. A spot showing Jordan swinging away got to storyboards, but given his batting average, it was later permanently shelved.

Although the spots weren't particularly memorable, the brand never really suffered. Jordan's name somehow remained gold in the endorsement world. During his time away from basketball, there wasn't even a noticeable dip in sales of Air Jordans.

Gatorade executives also were smart not to count on Jordan to carry the entire brand.

"Michael gave the brand a little bit more sex appeal and a lot more inspiration," said Sue Wellington, Gatorade's vice president of marketing, when Jordan retired for the first time. "But everyone was bright to never make him a one-trick pony. He was exceptionally important to the brand, but he was never the brand."

In early 1995, Gatorade ran a spot that featured Jordan running through a mountainous region to see a guru of sorts. He sat down with the guru and asked him about the meaning of life, and the guru responded with Gatorade's newest slogan, "Life is a sport. Drink it up." Many in the press thought that Gatorade had insight into the possibility of Jordan's return.

Sure enough, in March of 1995, Jordan announced that he would in fact be coming out of retirement and rejoining the Bulls. Gatorade would get a couple more years of basketball out of him. Over the next three full seasons, Jordan and the Bulls won another three championships. He did fewer Gatorade spots, averaging about two a year in the late 1990s, but he was still widely used as part of Gatorade's expansion into the international marketplace, where he provided instant credibility. Jordan also helped Gatorade gain valuable space in Wal-Mart stores across the country.

Following the Bulls' fourth championship in 1996, the Gatorade sales team was trying to get the much-coveted off-of-shelf displays with the largest retailer in the United States. They were aiming for the month of September, typically the last big month of Gatorade's nationwide sales every year. Wal-Mart officials told the Gatorade representatives that the only way they would be able to compete with the back-to-school aisle displays was to comply with Wal-Mart's number-one goal, "Retailtainment," a word the company had made up to convey that it wanted shopping to be fun.

That September, Gatorade got the displays it wanted. On the highly stacked Gatorade display was a cutout of Jordan that enabled shoppers to compare their hand and foot sizes with those of the basketball legend.

However, Jordan's greatest contribution to Gatorade in his second NBA stint was a real moment that happened with a large audience watching.

Gatorade had made its legend from genuine moments, and one of the best ones in brand lore came with Jordan on June 11, 1997. The Bulls and the Utah Jazz were tied at two games apiece in the NBA Finals, and Jordan had been battling the flu all day before the pivotal Game 5 in Salt Lake City, where the Jazz had won 23 straight games. He was sweating profusely and had been in bed all day. His eyes were clearly tired from the ordeal his body was going through.

But Jordan was still Jordan, and those watching the game might have believed that Gatorade was a part of his performance. On the bench, he was seen getting ice packs applied to the back of his neck while he swigged Gatorade—or what the *Miami Herald's* Dan LeBatard called Jordan's "miracle cure."[10] Jordan scored 21 points in the first half and 17 in the second and lifted the Bulls to a 90–88 victory.

"I almost played myself into passing out," Jordan told reporters after the game. "I couldn't breathe, my energy level was really low, my mouth was really dry. They just started giving me Gatorade, and they thought about an IV. But by the time they could get the IV, I was drinking enough fluids."[11]

In 1998, *Fortune* magazine estimated that Jordan had at least a $10 billion impact on the U.S. economy. That year, in what would be Jordan's last year with the Bulls, Gatorade brought back "Be Like Mike." While Gatorade's market share didn't increase significantly with Jordan, signing the most popular athlete in the world could have helped stop the growth of other entrants in the marketplace as the sports drink category grew exponentially.

"He was definitely high on the cool factor, and his signing did help the Gatorade brand image, but he certainly didn't make or break our business," said Jim Doyle, who worked on the Gatorade brand from 1991 to 1998. "It takes sales, distribution, and research and development as well as marketing to create a business success."

When Jordan retired for the second time, Gatorade was more prepared.

Quaker executives had already had discussions with women's soccer star Mia Hamm. And although Jordan's contract guaranteed that he'd be Gatorade's sole spokesman through 2001, Jordan said yes to the alliance. Hamm was a standout at Jordan's alma mater, the University of North Carolina.

Gatorade later added Indianapolis Colts quarterback Peyton Manning, Houston Rockets center Yao Ming, and New York Yankees shortstop Derek Jeter as well as Mia Hamm in what brand executives called "The Volkswagen" or "Beetle" strategy.

Officials with the brand knew that they couldn't return to having no athletes—sports marketing had changed drastically since 1985.

But they also realized that when Jordan retired, the one-athlete strategy wasn't going to continue to be relevant either. Jordan had no equal, and the people who worked on Gatorade wanted to have the ability to choose the athlete who was hot at the time to feature in the company's advertising. So they went with the "How many people can we fit in a buggy?" model. The idea was to alternate athletes to help pitch the brand.

"As part of the fabric of sports, we need to continue to evolve," Fox said. "We can't pick one horse and ride that horse till the end because consumers love athletes and they love their teams, but that encompasses a lot of different personalities."

In 1999, Sue Wellington, who was now president of Quaker Oats's U.S. beverage business, looked at the seven Gatorade ads that were planned for the year. Mia Hamm was not on the list.

"You've got to be kidding," Wellington said. "She's the best female athlete in the world, and we just signed her, and what the hell did we sign her for if we're not going to put her in an ad?"

Wellington then uttered words that will never be forgotten.

"Why don't we put her in an ad with Michael?" she said. The other executives stared at her, as if to say that no athlete deserved the screen with Michael.

"We weren't going to use her because she's not anywhere near the status of Michael Jordan," said Danny Schuman, who had been working on Gatorade advertising since 1991.

The result was Michael versus Mia; the ad featured Jordan versus Hamm in various sporting events. The spot was scored with a version of "Anything I Can Do, You Can Do Better."

"We thought we might be hurting Jordan's image," Schuman said. "She's 5-foot-5 and he's 6-foot-6. We wanted to make a believable commercial. And the success of the commercial, we owe in part to

Mia's performance. She was incredibly competitive. When the two raced each other at full speed, she actually beat Michael in a sprint."

Later that year, Hamm became a household name when the U.S. women won the women's World Cup in their home country. Gatorade, along with Nike, was most associated with Hamm.

"The ad put boys and girls, men and women, on the same level," said Andy Horrow, a current Gatorade executive who began his work on the brand in 1996. "People gave us credit for being the first to do something like that."

Thanks in part to Hamm, Gatorade officials now say that, among their youngest drinking audience, half are boys and half are girls.

"Gatorade is an amazing company to work for," Hamm said. "For so long, they had just Michael, and when they came and brought me in, I think it really helped our sport."

In 2001, Jordan came out of retirement for a second time, this time joining the Wizards in Washington, D.C., where he had served as part owner and president of basketball operations during his latest retirement. Jordan wasn't the same in his final run, but who could expect him to be? By the time he retired after a two-year stint, he was 40 years old. He still averaged 21.2 points a game, but he clearly didn't have the quality of teammates with the Wizards that he had had with the Bulls, and the team failed to make the playoffs in both years. Jordan wasn't as active in pitching Gatorade in his final playing years.

Brand managers believed that he was losing his on-court relevance and that the sports marketing model that he had helped pioneer was being overutilized by companies, minimizing the impact of any one athlete's relationship with a company. Gatorade had evolved past Michael Jordan, but executives certainly didn't forget about him. In 2001, they signed him through 2007.

In what might be the final tribute to the relationship, Gatorade ponied up more than $2 million to air its commercial "23 vs. 39" during the broadcast of Super Bowl XXXVII on January 26, 2003. The much-acclaimed spot, which arguably was Gatorade's most popular spot with Jordan aside from "Be Like Mike," featured a 23-year-old Michael Jordan versus the 39-year-old version in a game of one-on-one. A 1987 version of Jordan's head was digitally sculpted and inserted on a double playing the younger Jordan. In a comical twist, at the end of the commercial, an even younger, North Carolina version of Jordan asks if anyone has winners.

The goal of the ad spot wasn't to sell sports drinks, as "Be Like Mike" had done. It was meant to be a public "thank you" to Jordan for all he had given Gatorade over the years. But like "Be Like Mike," it will probably be ingrained in the minds of sports fans and avid Gatorade drinkers for a long time.

"Be Like Mike" is still quoted over and over again by sports marketers working in today's environment.

Before the 2002 Winter Olympic Games in Salt Lake City, Matt Mannelly—who moved on to become the chief marketing officer of the United States Olympic Committee (USOC)—was sitting in a boardroom when USOC executives were discussing how they were going to capitalize on their relationship with the apparel licensee Roots. The prevailing thought was that they didn't want to sell the exact apparel worn by the athletes before the games because they wanted the apparel to be special to the athletes. One person advocated making a green version available to the public, instead of the blue designated for the athletes.

"You guys don't get it," Mannelly said. "People want to 'Be Like Mike,' not 'Kind of Like Mike.'"

CHAPTER 7

"We're Going to War"

IN JANUARY 1992, Quaker and Coca-Cola were discussing the possibility of a joint venture. Gatorade was the king of the U.S. sports beverage market, but in order to grow the brand, Quaker needed to get it into vending machines and to exploit the international marketplace. Coca-Cola had an intricate worldwide system, with distribution channels already set up in 175 countries. Gatorade, at the time, was doing business in only 13 of those countries. Quaker's Gatorade business in Europe was struggling because the success of Quaker's European operations was based on disproportionate sales in cold countries, where hot oatmeal was popular. Gatorade is a drink that is consumed most in hot areas, so this went against Quaker's international distribution strength.

A joint venture with Quaker initially interested Coca-Cola officials because they were aware of Gatorade's potential. This was
despite the fact that the company was already competing with
Gatorade internationally. Its sports drink called Aquarius (which was
more of a leisure beverage than an efficacious rehydration drink) had
been rolled out in Japan in 1983 and had become as profitable in
Asia and Europe as Gatorade was in the United States. But Coca-
Cola did not have the trademark rights to the name Aquarius in the
United States. This was why Coca-Cola had not gone head-to-head
with Gatorade on the companies' native soil until its U.S. drink
POWERade was unveiled in fountain form in April 1990.

There were two major issues that needed to be resolved if the
partnership was going to work. One was that POWERade could not
be bottled and sold in stores. The other was a clause that stated that
once the venture was formed, if the partners could not agree on a
business plan in any given year, either company had the right to buy
out the other. At the time, Quaker's business was worth about $5 bil-
lion, approximately one-tenth the value of Coca-Cola. If Quaker
agreed to this clause, Coca-Cola could easily buy out Quaker at a
price that might be less than fair market value. Other than as an
acquisition threat, the clause meant little to Quaker because it certainly didn't have the wherewithal to buy out Coca-Cola. The buy-
out clause became the sticking point. A few weeks after Quaker
executives rejected the deal, Quaker's potential partner became its
chief competitor. POWERade was bottled and put in test markets,
and it was clear that, this time, there would be a nationwide rollout.

Coke and Pepsi Attack

In April 1992, the timing and quality of the product were finally
right for Coca-Cola.

"Coke had always been late," said Sergio Zyman, who was Coca-Cola's chief marketing officer at the time. "And we had this arrogance that was more of a blindness, to be honest. It was like General Motors. They said to themselves, 'We're selling big cars; that's what the consumer wants; nobody is going to buy the foreign cars made out of plastic,' but they did."

Coke introduced Mello Yello only after Mountain Dew was successful. It introduced Mr. Pibb after the success of Dr. Pepper, Frutopia after Snapple made waves, and KMX following Red Bull's development of the energy-drink market.

Coke had previously tried its hand at introducing an American sports drink and had failed. The company had sponsored the Olympics since 1930, and in 1970 it unveiled Olympade. The can had the familiar Olympic rings on it and featured the red, white, and blue associated with the American flag. Unfortunately for Coke, Olympade was never marketed well enough for the drink to make it to the 1972 Olympics in Munich.

"Gatorade identified and developed the market—and while everyone was looking at the growth of Gatorade, the market wasn't all that big at the time," said Dr. Jon Frieden, who was Coca-Cola's marketing research supervisor during the Olympade rollout. "Olympade's test market started and ended in Birmingham, Alabama, and it was never sold anywhere else."

Coca-Cola's next attempt came in 1984 at the Summer Olympics in Los Angeles. This time, Coke tried to leverage its sponsorship by giving athletes a product called Hi-C Thirst Quencher. But the drink tasted so bad that the liaison responsible for taking care of the athletes purchased cases of Gatorade for the participants in the games to drink. (It was unclear whether the liaison thought that the athletes were used to Gatorade or believed that the drink would help the athletes, perform better.)

A year after the Olympics, Coca-Cola made another effort by licensing a drink called Max Energy and Fluid Replacement Drink, a citrus-flavored drink sold as a concentrate. Test markets in health clubs and gyms in Houston and Denver weren't successful. The biggest problem was that Coca-Cola had plenty of credibility among the masses, but, unlike Gatorade, it had no credibility among the athletes who would be the potential consumers of these products.

By 1992, the soft drink market was worth approximately $40 billion, while the sports drink market was on an upward climb toward $1 billion. While the sports drink market seemed small, it was growing faster, and it had greater potential for profit. Gatorade essentially sold for twice as much as a similar volume of Coke and used half the amount of sugar (the expensive ingredient) that soft drinks did. Sports drinks were also starting to emerge as a casual drink, appearing at occasions that would otherwise be reserved for a soda.

By the time POWERade reached shelves, Pepsi already had its product out, Mountain Dew Sport. Many thought that the powerful push of the two soft drink giants (Pepsi also owned Frito-Lay, which had a significant presence at retail) would push Gatorade to the back of the refrigerator. Coke and Pepsi crushed Gatorade in terms of total volume. In fact, more bottles of Coca-Cola were sold in 1925 than bottles of Gatorade in 1991. And Coke and Pepsi had superior distribution systems that were used to overpowering and undercutting local and regional brands. They were refined by competing against each other.

"If Pepsi-Cola didn't exist, I would try to invent it," Roberto Goizueta, Coca-Cola's chief executive from 1981 to 1997, once said. "It keeps us, and them, on our toes and keeps us lean."[1]

On the surface, it appeared that Coke and Pepsi's distribution model, which involved direct-to-store delivery, with dedicated truckers showing up at the stores and stocking shelves every day, would blow away Gatorade's model of shipping to stores through food brokers acting as sales agents.

"We had a lot of confidence in our consumer proposition and our brand equity, but they brought a whole set of advantages from a direct store delivery perspective and what we thought would be really deep consumer pocketbooks that would be a challenge for us," said Cindy Alston, a longtime Gatorade executive.

The equity of the Gatorade name was indeed powerful. The brand had a larger share of the U.S. sports drink market (83 percent) at the time than Coke and Pepsi combined had of the soft drink market. It also had the advantage of being known as the first in the thirst-quencher business.

"The winners are those companies that introduce new brands that create new categories," wrote branding and marketing experts Al and Laura Ries. "The Gatorades, not the POWERades. The Mountain Dews, not the Mello Yellos. The Dr. Peppers, not the Mr. Pibbs."[2]

But other business originators had been challenged and lost a major part of their market share because they failed to evolve. Such was the case with Polaroid, a company that had revolutionized photography with the instantaneous photo. But in large part as a result of digital cameras, the company lost its relevance. Gatorade was able to hold off the big boys because its management team strategically exploited the weaknesses of the soft drink model, while building up the brand's own strengths.

"I looked those who I managed in the eye and said, 'We will win this battle with Coke and Pepsi, and we will win it with our brains, not our brawn,'" said David Williams, who was vice president of broker sales at the time.

Coke and Pepsi attacked Gatorade out in the open through advertising, while Gatorade's most valuable strikes were its attacks on Coke and Pepsi behind the scenes.

Both Coca-Cola and Pepsi told consumers that their drinks tasted better than Gatorade. Going with the taste tactic was not unfamiliar ground—the two companies had been doing this for years. In the late 1970s and early 1980s, for example, Pepsi filmed blind taste tests and used them as advertising. Partly as a result of the Pepsi Challenge, Coca-Cola discontinued its main brand and brought out New Coke in 1985. The public strongly rejected New Coke, and the classic formula soon replaced it.

Coca-Cola's POWERade did in fact have more sugar than Gatorade. Coke claimed that this formula would give the consumer more available energy and thus make the drink more effective than Gatorade. It used an 8 percent sugar solution compared to Gatorade's 6 percent mixture. Gatorade officials fired back through the media, saying that POWERade, from a scientific standpoint, didn't have enough sodium and might have too many carbohydrates, which would slow the passage of the solution through the body and cause cramping. Coca-Cola officials were sure that the 2 percent difference in carbohydrates didn't slow absorption, and that if their drink did in fact taste better, people who were sweating would be willing to drink more of it when they were dehydrated.

The "taste better" line might have worked with a soft drink, but perhaps it was less effective with a sports drink. Gatorade had the science behind it to prove to the consumer that Gatorade worked. Coca-Cola didn't have the same body of research.

"Gatorade had become part of the athlete's work ethic," said sports psychotherapist Dr. Rick Aberman of the Lennick Aberman

Group, a performance consulting firm in Minneapolis, Minnesota. "It might have not tasted the best, but the perception was that it was something you just do as an athlete to make things work. I'm sure many athletes thought, 'If this POWERade stuff tastes like Kool-Aid, how can it work as well?' Or, 'POWERade, that's for wimps who can't get used to Gatorade.'"

Coke and Pepsi then resolved to do what they did best—price wars. In the early part of the 20th century, Pepsi made strides against Coca-Cola by selling twice as much for the same price—12-ounce bottles for a nickel. So Pepsi and Coke decided to sell their products cheaply and in some cases give retailers free cases. For a 14-year-old kid using his lunch money to buy a drink for his after-school activities, the 20-cent difference between Pepsi and Coke's entries and Gatorade might have made it worth giving the newcomer a try. But the price difference wasn't enough to stifle interest in Gatorade.

For Coca-Cola and Pepsi, there was a negative effect from the soft drink pricing wars.

"Coke and Pepsi had made themselves generic products through pricing," Williams said. "The customer would simply pick whatever brand was the most discounted. We believed that it was not a pricing formula. It was a price-value formula. No one performed better than us, so our product was still worth what you paid for it."

Coca-Cola and Pepsi also supposedly had an advantage because they basically owned refrigerator doors in convenience stores top to bottom. But that division of products hurt POWERade and Mountain Dew Sport, which was later renamed All Sport, because these drinks were in the same compartment as the companies' soft drinks, separating them from Gatorade and making it harder for a potential consumer to do a head-to-head price comparison.

Gatorade officials found that they could not only survive but remain on top while methodically neutralizing the strengths of the soda giants like no brand ever had done.

The soft drink companies had incredible distribution, but their system was based on having only a few products on their trucks. Gatorade managers made it a priority to come out with as many flavors as possible, knowing that the bottlers of Coke and Pepsi, who were used to making only a few drinks, would have to get used to more complexity if they were to give their consumers the same number of flavor options. Over the next eight years, Gatorade introduced 16 new flavors in the United States, after having only six flavors in its first 25 years of existence.

Even if Coca-Cola and Pepsi matched Gatorade's flavor proliferation (which they didn't), those who were delivering product would have to find a way to make room for all those flavors on their trucks, which were already crammed with soft drinks.

"We knew that these truck drivers were often paid on a commission basis," said Jim Doyle, who was named president of Gatorade worldwide in April 1992. "If a Coke driver was putting POWERade on his truck, he was taking off cases of Coke, and if a Pepsi driver was putting All Sport on his truck, he was not delivering as much Pepsi. The product wasn't going to move as fast, so how many guys do you think were willing to put more sports drinks on their truck?"

Gatorade officials also discovered over the years that while Coke and Pepsi had national distribution, their distribution had holes, which limited their market share in certain parts of the country. This manifested itself in the local market metrics. In Coke's strongholds in the southeast, POWERade would have 18 percent of the market, with All Sport taking 2 percent. Where Pepsi was strong, the numbers would be flipped to All Sport's advantage. This helped to calm the fears of those working on Gatorade. While many people had talked about Coca-Cola and Pepsi's national distribution dominance, it was really a web of regional dominances that was split and spread out across the country.

Some other perceived advantages were never factors. One of these was Pepsi's stake in the restaurant business. With its ownership of Pizza Hut, Taco Bell, and Kentucky Fried Chicken, Pepsi had more restaurants than any other company in the world. If the company forced the restaurants to put the drink in their systems, and if the product was good, it would serve as a perfect introduction of the product to consumers, who might then look for the bottled product in stores. But fountain space was too precious, and All Sport never had enough market share to warrant taking away a stalwart brand in order to stock it.

Even including Pepsi's restaurants, Coca-Cola's fountain presence outnumbered Pepsi's fountain space by a three-to-one margin in the United States.[3] By the mid-1990s, Coca-Cola had secured the pouring rights in at least 20 stadiums in all four major sports. But Gatorade officials never wanted their drink in a fountain in these settings because it would distort the positioning of the product, which was based on athletic instead of culinary occasions.

All Sport Dismantled

Mountain Dew Sport was an easier product to fend off than POWERade. Pepsi might have had dual-sport athlete Bo Jackson wrestling an alligator, a symbol of its top competition, in an ad that proclaimed that Mountain Dew Sport "puts back what sports take out," but the drink—despite its label—was not formulated to be consumed during sporting events. Gatorade officials were encouraged when tests that they had done showed that Pepsi's attempt at a carbonated sports drink had produced throat burn and other nuisances in athletes trying to chug the product.

But, to their credit, Gatorade executives knew that they had to take Pepsi's entry seriously, and they advertised in Pepsi's test markets aggressively in a very public way. They produced coupons in those test markets and ran ads that were termed "physiology versus fizziology," playing off the fact that Pepsi's drink was carbonated.

"We had incredible respect for PepsiCo, since they were the very best," said Peter Vitulli, who was managing Gatorade's U.S. business during Mountain Dew Sport's launch in 1991. "That's why we felt that if we didn't do the right things, they were going to eat our lunch."

Gatorade then produced local commercials to be featured in each of Mountain Dew Sport's test markets. The most inflammatory one ran in Minnesota.

The spot featured Vikings head trainer Fred Zamberletti, who talked about the benefits of Gatorade and the cons of Mountain Dew Sport. Zamberletti asked the viewers whether they preferred a sports drink made by a soft drink company or a sports drink created for athletes. The end of the commercial had Zamberletti crushing the Mountain Dew Sport can and throwing it into the garbage. Pepsi eventually changed the name of the drink to All Sport, mostly because consumers didn't want to think of a soda when they bought a sports drink. The branding didn't help much—it was still carbonated.

Gatorade also had to focus on making sure that Coke and Pepsi didn't take away its position as the sideline beverage in its key professional sports. Although they hadn't marketed sports beverages on a national level before, both soft drink companies had plenty of experience in using sports figures to try to boost product sales.

Roger Enrico, president and chief executive of Pepsi's worldwide beverage division, happened to be a former assistant brand manager for Wheaties and loved using jocks in commercials. Coca-Cola had always realized the value of tying its soft drink to athletes. Detroit Tigers great Ty Cobb even pitched Coke as a thirst quencher of sorts.

"On days when we are playing a double header, I always find that a drink of Coca-Cola between the games refreshes me to an extent that I can start the second game feeling as if I had not been exercising at all," Cobb is quoted as saying in a 1906 print advertisement.[4]

In 1913, Coca-Cola advertised on 25 million baseball cards. In 1952, the company put a Coca-Cola cooler in the Russian compound in the athletes' Olympic village in Helsinki and snapped photos of athletes drinking its product.

One of Coke's most talked about commercials was its 1980 spot with Pittsburgh Steelers defensive tackle "Mean" Joe Greene. The ad, in which the intimidating Greene, limping toward the locker room, interacts with a young boy who offers him a Coke and eventually gets Greene's jersey, won worldwide acclaim. However, the ad was eventually pulled by Sergio Zyman, citing the fact that sales in the United States were flat, even as the creativity of the commercial continued to be hyped.

Along the same lines, Gatorade officials had to remember that the bottom line was to sell product, not to be called the official sports drink of every organization at any cost.

"We realized that competition would mean that we could continue to [pay more for official sponsorship relationships]," Doyle said. "But we realized that we had to become good at walking away if we couldn't make the numbers work."

Gatorade executives determined that it was worth it to buy category exclusivity on NBC during the 1992 Olympics so that Coca-Cola—which was paying $35 million to be called an official Olympics sponsor—couldn't advertise POWERade on the air. In 1996, Coca-Cola returned the favor by guaranteeing that Gatorade couldn't appear on U.S. Olympics TV broadcasts.

Gatorade had locked up many colleges and universities, but when Coca-Cola came in, the company didn't spend foolishly to make sure its beverage was on the sidelines everywhere. So POWERade became the sideline beverage of the Florida State Seminoles, the Auburn Tigers, and the Michigan State Spartans, among many others. Pepsi's sponsorship of the NCAA put All Sport on coolers in 1994, and Coca-Cola's high bid made POWERade the official sports drink of the 1996 World Cup.

"By buying the rights to serve Gatorade on the sidelines of professional basketball and football games, the brand receives more credibility than any television ad could provide, as it is shown under the radar in a real, unpaid-for setting, right on national television," wrote Jonathan Bond and Richard Kirshenbaum of the innovative marketing firm Kirshenbaum Bond + Partners.

> Consumers have become so cynical that they not only know sports celebrities are being paid to endorse products, they even know how much. During every TV game, TV cameras find the pros drinking the product in bright Gatorade-branded cups—and it is obvious they are doing it because they truly like the product, not because their agents told them to. If we handled the competitor, Powerade, we would urge it to do less advertising and pay the sports leagues whatever it takes to get the contract away from Gatorade once it expires.[5]

But Gatorade made sure to pony up big bucks for its key properties—the NFL and the NBA.

"They are the most athletic of products, and they have used their association with major professional sports to maintain that image," said NBA commissioner David Stern. "They have activated across a wide array of programs from product placement to sponsorships, and they do it as well as any company that we do business with."

Gatorade didn't make a counteroffer when Coca-Cola reportedly committed $30 million in 1997 for a four-year deal with the National Hockey League, where its coolers would be the less visible than in any other of the four major professional sports.

Gatorade's brand managers didn't get into a bidding war with Coca-Cola and Pepsi when it came to signing athletes. Gatorade's contract with Michael Jordan legally prevented Quaker officials from signing a stable of athletes to represent the brand and box out the competition. They didn't need to do that. In 1994, Coca-Cola signed the modern-day Bo Jackson, Deion Sanders, to pitch POWERade, while Orlando Magic center Shaquille O'Neal pitched All Sport. The two were second-rate compared to Jordan.

"Who are you going to put up against Michael Jordan to say, 'Well, I drink POWERade, so you ought to, too?'" questioned brand consultant Rick Kash. "It really was the final nail in the competitive defense."[6]

Gatorade mobilized Jordan by running an ad with Bulls trainer Chip Schaefer, who lists the benefits of Gatorade while Jordan practices in the background. The tagline in the commercial was "Nothing Beats Gatorade."

Jordan also gave the brand a huge boost internationally, perhaps more so than in the United States. He was truly a worldwide icon, and in those markets that were seeing Gatorade for the first time, having Jordan was enough for some consumers.

In October 1993, Gatorade was launched in Australia—a place where the ultimate thirst quencher previously was beer. Thanks to Jordan, Gatorade had a 40 percent share of the sports-drink market in about a month's time. But when Coca-Cola's international distribution machine came to the country in the summer of 1995, it overtook Gatorade as the market leader within a year.

Realizing that Gatorade's heritage was its strong point, something that Australian consumers didn't know about, those in charge of the Gatorade marketing in Australia produced a 2½-minute documentary about Gatorade's origin that ran as advertising. The spot featured Dr. Cade, former University of Florida quarterback Steve Spurrier, former coach Ray Graves, and former Gators cheerleader Donna Kay Berger, among others, who helped tell the story of Gatorade's beginnings through original commentary and old video.

Within a month's time, consumer tracking studies revealed that awareness of Gatorade outnumbered awareness of POWERade by a margin of 30 percent, with 74 percent saying that the advertising was meaningful to them.[7] Gatorade eventually took the lead again.

Years later, Gatorade officials realized that most of the United States didn't know Gatorade's story. Furthermore, Gatorade's advertising firm, Element 79, was hoping to communicate a "better than water" message because consumers were buying more bottled water at the time. So it produced smaller versions of the Australian ad and chose famous college football announcer Keith Jackson to narrate it.

Back in the United States in the mid-1990s, Pepsi and Coca-Cola tried to undercut Gatorade through lower prices and pitching their products' sweeter taste. But Quaker officials approved greater marketing spending, which forced the big boys to step up.

"All we did was copy the Budweiser strategy," Doyle said. "We're going to spend, so you're going to have to spend more to keep up with us." About 30 cents of every dollar went back into marketing or sales. This strategy also helped knock out the smaller players in the business, such as Suntory's 10-K. This product was competing with Gatorade in the early 1990s, and it had achieved some success in Louisiana and Mississippi with a large advertising budget in these areas. But when Coca-Cola and Pepsi came in, Gatorade and its two national competitors were spending so much money that Suntory could no longer hope to eventually achieve national relevance for 10-K, given the greater buy-in costs.

Gatorade executives mastered the strategy of when and where to advertise. Once they figured this out, their advertising was as prevalent as Coke and Pepsi's advertising for their core brands. This was accomplished by matching the advertising budgets of the soft drink giants during the summer months, when the most Gatorade was sold.

"If you watched during that seasonal period when Gatorade was important, you saw as much Gatorade advertising as you did Coke and Pepsi advertising," said Phil Marineau, who at the time was president of Quaker Oats. "That gave us the ability to break through, and it wasn't just our $500 million brand versus their multi-billion-dollar brand." Much of that strategy still applies today, as Gatorade spends approximately 80 percent of its marketing dollars in spring and summer. During the other months, Gatorade spends money in Sunbelt cities that are hot year-round.

By the end of 1995, Gatorade's share of the market had fallen by more than 20 percent in a decade. Between 1993 and 1995, the brand's share slipped to 72.3 percent, while All Sport had 9.8 percent and POWERade took a 12.1 percent piece of the pie.[8] This might have sounded bad, but the loss came at a time where Pepsi and Coca-Cola were devoting a tremendous amount of resources to beating Gatorade. The next couple of years would be critical in determining whether the two soft drink powers could ever become steady competitors of Gatorade.

1996 Olympics

Brand officials continued to work hard at every chance they got. In July 1996, Bill Schmidt walked into a health club near the house he was renting for the Summer Olympics in Atlanta. The woman at the door greeted Schmidt and, after a brief conversation, learned that he was in charge of sports marketing for Gatorade. She asked him if the company would do a sponsorship with the club and provide it with much-needed towels. It wasn't the kind of deal that Schmidt usually did, but it came at a time when Gatorade was trying to mobilize in Coca-Cola's hometown. As an added bonus, Schmidt knew that many Coca-Cola executives worked out at the facility, including Zyman.

"It gave me great joy knowing that he couldn't use the towels there because they had Gatorade logos on them," said the always competitive Schmidt.

At the time, Coca-Cola was spending an estimated $250 million on Olympics-based television commercials and promotions, some of which was devoted to POWERade. The company reportedly paid $350,000 to support Atlanta in its Olympics bid and ponied up $12 million to sponsor a cross-country torch relay. More than 7,000 police officers had special holsters to hold their sports drink bottles.

It was one big Coca-Cola pride party, with the Olympics being held in the hometown of the company's headquarters.

"Coca-Cola made a huge push with POWERade during the Olympics in 1996, in order to make a significant dent in Gatorade's share, and they couldn't do it," said John Sicher, editor and publisher of *Beverage Digest*. "Gatorade was just too strong."

In October 1997, when Robert Morrison arrived from Kraft Foods to take over as Quaker's chairman and chief executive officer, he said of Gatorade, "I can tell you that what's built the brand is marketing."[9] While marketing did help build the brand, marketing wasn't the only thing that was going to sustain Gatorade's dominant market share.

Convenience Store Strategy

Part of the reason why Coca-Cola was having such trouble gaining additional market share was because Gatorade officials, over a period of six years, had finally mastered the art of selling to convenience stores—a group of businesses with typically less than 5,000 square feet, many of which stay open 24 hours a day, 7 days a week.

In the early 1990s, Gatorade's sales-management team realized that the food brokers that Gatorade used were selling the product to grocery store retailers effectively, but that they had not been paying attention to the convenience stores.

To be fair, few food and beverage manufacturers had devoted much time to the convenience stores. They were considered more of an auxiliary food and beverage retailer, along with drugstores and mass merchandisers, since each convenience store was selling only about $660 in noncarbonated beverages in 1987.

But Gatorade officials felt that convenience stores were a rapidly growing segment of the business. With gas station mini-marts popping up across the country, the number of convenience stores in the United States topped 100,000 for the first time in 1987. They also knew that their product was most often purchased on a single-serving, spur-of-the-moment basis, which was essentially the business model of the convenience stores.

In the early 1990s, the team started working hard on this segment. First, they found out how these stores worked. Most of them had one refrigerator door reserved for Pepsi, another reserved for Coke products, and a third reserved for the local bottler. The rest of the cooler doors were supplied through wholesalers, and there didn't seem to be any organized plan for effective allocation of shelf space.

So Gatorade took its team of 60 food brokers, who acted as independent agents, and built the capability of calling on more than a thousand convenience store headquarters, including 7-Eleven, Circle K, and White Hen Pantry. Simultaneously, the company put together a team of people to make weekly contact with more than 50,000 of the top-volume retail chain stores nationwide. This was the first attempt ever made by a non-direct-to-store-delivery business to effectively sell the convenience store channel from top to bottom.

The food brokers were automatically motivated to make things work with Gatorade. They were building a new channel capability in convenience stores. As the Gatorade business grew, they could turn to other manufacturers and use Gatorade as an example of what they could do for those manufacturers' brands. It was a marriage made in heaven.

"They were indebted to us because we had created a new revenue stream for them," Williams said. "Not only did we introduce them to the channel, but we helped to underwrite their initial costs, developed sales call patterns, and conducted training sessions for all of their people."

The food brokers were in fact rewarded when Campbell's unveiled its carrot juice mixes—V8 Splash—in 1997. It hired all the brokers that worked with Gatorade.

Gatorade officials took things a step further by teaching retailers how to sell in their convenience stores. Williams sat on the education committee of the National Association of Convenience Stores (NACS) and would often give seminars on what Gatorade knew about the emerging business. The talk was backed up with research—cameras inside convenience stores recorded how long an average consumer stayed in a store and the usual path taken by a customer inside the store. This key data was appreciated by convenience store managers, who used the information to place their most profitable products, which not coincidentally often included Gatorade, in high-traffic areas.

"Coke and Pepsi sold with their brawn," Williams said. "They'd load you up and tell you how much you were getting. They treated the convenience store like a little stepchild. We went in and taught the retailers how people buy beverages so that they could use that information to build volume and profits."

Sometimes the results of Gatorade's research surprised retailers. One study showed that consumers in the convenience store setting were more likely to buy Gatorade priced at two bottles for $3 than they were if the bottles cost 99 cents each. This went against the traditional idea that the lower the price, the more consumers would buy. This "promotion" yielded the retailer $1.50 per Gatorade, while at the single-bottle price, only 99 cents was coming into the cash register. It wasn't that the people at Gatorade were trying to help the convenience store get the most money out of their customers, but studies like these showed convenience store retailers that they didn't know as much as they thought they knew about the people who were buying their products.

"Soon every convenience store had to have three items—*Playboy* and *Penthouse*, Marlboro cigarettes, and Gatorade," Marineau said. When convenience stores thought about the reallocation of shelf space, they often called the people on Gatorade's sales team for advice—a fact that must have made executives at Coke and Pepsi cringe.

From 1991 to 1996, sales of noncarbonated beverages in convenience stores rose an average of 96.1 percent, and by 1999, total sales of sports drinks in convenience stores topped $1 billion.[10] Four years later, each store was selling an average of $10,941 in sports drinks per year and convenience stores led all retail channels in sales of sports drinks, accounting for 34 percent of total sports drink sales, surpassing sales of sports drinks in supermarkets (28 percent), drugstores (13 percent), mass merchandisers (10 percent), and health and natural food stores (7 percent).[11]

"[Those working on Gatorade] actually became better at representing and delivering Gatorade in the sports drink market than Coca-Coca was in the soft drink market," said Michael Bellas of the Beverage Marketing Corporation, who charted Gatorade's growth through the decades.

After an all-time low market share of 72 percent in 1996, Gatorade's share rose to 76.1 percent by the end of 1999. POWERade's share rose to an all-time high of 16 percent at the expense of All Sport, which had all but been reduced to a niche player. Despite their size and their capital, Coca-Cola and Pepsi never spent more than Gatorade on marketing their sports drinks. The $81 million Quaker spent on advertising in 1999 was five times as much as Coca-Cola spent on POWERade and 275 times as much as Pepsi devoted to All Sport.[12]

No matter how good the system that Gatorade set up was, the brand would not have achieved the amount of success it did if it hadn't sold through retailers. Not only did it sell, it was considered enough of a unique item that it hardly ever had to reduce prices in order to compete, so retailers were making full margin on the product all the time.

"I don't think anyone drinking Gatorade thought that their mere drinking of it cemented their status as an athlete," said sports sociologist Dr. Jay Coakley, author of *Sport in Society: Issues and Controversies.* "But products are connected with your identity as an athlete, and one of the crucial factors of identity is authenticity. Gatorade is, without a doubt, seen as the most authentic sports drink, to a point where people have come to expect it in a sports setting, to the point where its presence is taken for granted."

The feeling inside the beverage industry was that Coca-Cola would have tried harder and spent more money if it had believed it could make more headway against Gatorade. The year before, for example, the company had earmarked $1.8 billion to go to its bottlers, 66 percent of which was spent on the Coca-Cola brand alone.

Zyman, who today runs his own consulting firm in Atlanta, says that Coca-Cola executives never thought they could knock off Gatorade. "From the get-go, we knew our potential was limited," Zyman said. "We didn't think we'd get a large piece of the market. Our distribution system allowed us to get to home plate with a chance to bat, but that's about it, and in the end you still have to swing at the ball."

In 2000, it became clear that acquisition of Quaker Oats was the only way Pepsi or Coca-Cola would control the No. 1 U.S. sports drink position. By November, Coca-Cola chairman Douglas Daft was reportedly willing to agree to have the company pay almost $16 billion. But influential board member Warren Buffett reportedly said that giving up 10.5 percent of the Coca-Cola Company for Quaker was too much. He said he believed that the Gatorade acquisition would increase Coke's worldwide sales by only a very small margin and would burden Coca-Cola with Quaker's food business. Coca-Cola didn't necessarily want Quaker's food brands, so the deal was off.

Getting involved with Quaker Oats was easier to rationalize from Pepsi's standpoint, since the company was already in the food business thanks to owning Frito-Lay. Quaker Oats's other assets were therefore closer to Pepsi's core business than they were to Coke's. There was also a feeling at Pepsi that there was a great future in noncarbonated drinks. In October, Pepsi purchased the noncarbonated health drink brand SoBe for a reported $370 million. On December 4, 2000, it also emerged as the winning bidder for Quaker Oats, in exchange for $13.4 billion in stock.

As part of the terms of sale, Gatorade officials had to convince the Federal Trade Commission that the deal would not destroy competition in the sports drink marketplace. Pepsi sold All Sport to a small beverage company called Monarch to avoid having to sell two sports drinks and agreed not to put Gatorade in its distribution system for 10 years, except for vending machines and schools.

But Coca-Cola had spent an enormous amount of money to get a 16 percent share of the U.S. market. In addition to the cost of developing and marketing the product, producing it was another large expense. Producing POWERade forced Coca-Cola to spend money to build plants that could endure the hot-fill process that noncarbonated drinks required. Packaging was also a challenge in the hot-fill process, so more money had to be spent on plastic that could resist warping from the heat.

Given the costs that Coca-Cola had incurred to become a weak No. 2 competitor to Gatorade, analysts weren't convinced that the company had made the right decision when it passed on the Quaker Oats acquisition.

"I'm not sure Coke was right when they decided not to buy Gatorade," said Henry Asher, president of investment firm Northstar Group. "It would take decades to take the lead in the market, and the cost would not come cheaply."[13]

POWERade Relaunch

After passing up the chance to own Gatorade, Coca-Cola officials were ready to respond. They brought in a young, hip marketer named Rohan Oza, who had run urban marketing for Coca-Cola's Sprite brand for three years. The day after the Pepsi deal was announced, Oza told Jeff Dunn, the president and CEO of Coca-Cola North America, that he had a POWERade relaunch plan. In a matter of months, Oza changed the logo and added vitamins B3, B6, and B12, which the company claimed aided in energy metabolism. Gatorade officials said that their studies proved that all those vitamins did was provide drinkers with more vitamin B, which had no qualities linked to immediate energy metabolism. Gatorade later put vitamin B in its fitness water Propel, but only as part of a good-for-you positioning. To this day, those at the Gatorade Sports Science Institute assert that there is no physiological or performance benefit to having the vitamin in a sports drink.

Aside from their vitamin B claims, Coca-Cola officials hoped to establish more credibility with a better stable of athletes. POWERade signed Atlanta Falcons rookie Michael Vick and tennis player Andy Roddick and launched a catchy campaign, which received unprecedented attention in Coke's short history in sports drinks.

The spots, entitled "Very Real Power," were created by Wieden + Kennedy, the firm that had dreamed up countless ad classics for Nike and ESPN. The idea of the ads was to use camera angles and amateur-quality footage to make the viewer wonder if the ridiculous action that was taking place was real.

In Roddick's spot, he hits a serve so hard that it actually sticks in the clay. In Vick's commercial, the quarterback throws a ball almost 200 yards into the upper deck of a stadium. The discussion over whether these things really happened resulted in the most buzz POWERade had ever received.

At a presentation at a high school, students were invited to ask questions of Vick. One of the first questions he was asked was if he really threw the ball that far. Everyone in the crowd knew what the kid asking the question was talking about. Vick, as instructed by Coca-Cola officials, didn't tip his hand.

In a notebook column, *Sports Illustrated* reporters wrote that Vick's pass attempt was probably not real and that the longest throw is believed to have been made by Bears quarterback Rudy Bukich during a practice in the 1960s.[14]

Oza said that he believed that the drink's relaunch enabled many young people to perceive POWERade as "fresh and irreverent," whereas Gatorade was seen as "their father's drink." Gatorade officials maintained that their brand, as their science showed, was hardly outdated.

Public perception was very important to Oza. In one of his first public statements, Oza called Gatorade the "Goliath" and Coke the "David," something that surely must have seemed like a joke to many Quaker executives who were shivering in their boots when Coke entered the market in 1992.

"We're going to war," Oza told *Brandweek*, half jokingly. "We will have an air attack and ground attack. If we just do a ground attack we will get annihilated from the air. We have great grassroots prop-erties. Gatorade's going down. They are extremely confident. We have a team that knows exactly what they're doing."[15]

POWERade pushed Gatorade. It tried to appeal to kids and mothers by becoming the first to be sold in packs of six 12-ounce bottles, something that Gatorade might not otherwise have done because the expense of the plastic might outweigh what the brand could sell in volume. Even so, Gatorade soon followed with All-Stars, bottles of similar size in different Gatorade flavors.

Coca-Cola worked hard to give its consumers options. POWERade tried to appeal to the young crowd by launching drinks in nontraditional colors and giving them names that were slightly more hip than the Gatorade variety—Mountain Blast, Green Squall, and Jagged Ice, among others.

But by the end of 2002, it had become clear just how entrenched Gatorade was. In a four-year period with what was considered its most aggressive and successful marketing, POWERade had gained less than one point of market share in the United States. Gatorade, for the first time since 1993, had more than an 80 percent share of the market.

"The bottom line was that Coke and Pepsi had been watching us for so long and they never had a product to compete with us," said Marineau, who left the Gatorade brand in fall of 1995 after a 23-year career at Quaker Oats. "And by the time they were ready to compete, we were ready for them."

The marketing battle between the two reached its height in 2003 and 2004.

In August 2003, Coca-Cola signed No. 1 overall draft pick LeBron James to pitch its Sprite and POWERade brands. The 19-year-old James was hailed as the next coming of Michael Jordan. Although James had become the first player to win Gatorade's High School

Boys Basketball Player of the Year award twice, Gatorade executives contended that they were happy to pass on the deal, which, at $2 million per year, was above their price point for any one athlete.

They had gone to the "Volkswagen strategy," and by doing so had committed to featuring a group of athletes in the company's advertising. If Gatorade didn't want to abandon this model, it couldn't break the bank on James.

"Our model is such that we've evolved beyond using one individual athlete," said Tom Fox. "We need to be able to—at any given time—go in and present to the consumer an athlete who may be resonating at that particular moment in time. It's not about the individual athlete strategy."

Coca-Cola saw James as its chance to make another dent in Gatorade's armor. As an incentive to do the deal, James's agents, Aaron and Eric Goodwin, structured the contract so that if James helped grow POWERade's market share, James would get a percentage of the sales.

"It's very hard to out-Gatorade Gatorade," Bellas said. "Coke has done as well as they could have hoped for, but when you are number two, you have to look at trying to do things differently."

Not only did Coca-Cola need the powerful and relevant athlete, it needed a way to counteract the mystique that Gatorade had established. It tried to do that through the "Very Real Power" advertising campaign.

In 2004, POWERade made a "Very Real Power" spot of James swishing full-court shots with ease. Coca-Cola again caused a stir with the spot, which was filmed as if it had been taken by a personal videocamera. Viewers debated whether the advertisement was real, and Coca-Cola wisely didn't answer. The spot was named the eighth best sports advertisement of the year by the *Philadelphia Enquirer*.

James at least didn't disappoint on the court. In April 2004, he won the NBA's Rookie of the Year Award and joined Jordan and Oscar Robertson as the only players in league history to average more than 20 points, 5 rebounds, and 5 assists per game in their rookie season.

After James's first season, POWERade came out with FLAVA23, a "sourberry" concoction that had an animated James on the bottle. Consumers could also redeem labels for one of four James comic books, featuring James chugging POWERade at key moments in the comic book's plot.

Despite Coca-Cola's innovative moves, Gatorade officials tried to remind the public that their drink was about performance, not gimmicks.

"People aren't running around in a panic here," said Gatorade spokesman Andy Horrow. "Real athletes who need to hydrate don't buy a drink because an athlete is on the bottle, they buy a drink because of what's in the bottle."[16]

The key point of tension between the two brands came on the court, where 28 of the 30 NBA teams, *including* James's Cleveland Cavaliers, had a marketing deal with Gatorade. Since James was seen as the most important face of POWERade, he was not drinking out of the Gatorade waxed cups and was not using the towels stamped with the Gatorade logo. Unable to drink from POWERade bottles because of Gatorade's deal with the team, James would drink water out of unlabeled bottles or would put a sleeve that looked like a Cleveland Cavaliers jersey over the bottle. He would often have a clean white towel to dry off with when he got back to the bench.

The Goodwins, who James fired after the 2004-2005 season, said that despite a couple of bumps, Coke and the NBA seemed happy.

NASCAR Battleground

Gatorade and POWERade battled even more overtly on the marketing front in NASCAR.

After 18 years of being the official drink of NASCAR, Gatorade gave up that title to POWERade in 2002. NASCAR's deal gave the official sports drink a presence in victory lane, but Gatorade officials believed that the dynamic had changed, since the value did not lie with the governing body, but with the drivers themselves. Since NASCAR drivers are technically independent contractors, they have the right to structure their own marketing partnerships apart from those of the governing body. So Gatorade spent a considerable amount of money signing drivers like Ryan Newman, Mark Martin, Matt Kenseth, and Jimmie Johnson. It also debuted the "Gatorade In-Car Drinking System" (G.I.D.S.). This provided 100 ounces of cold Gatorade to the driver, who no longer had to squeeze a bottle while driving at high speeds. The fluid flows freely when the driver bites down on a tube, so the driver can drink throughout the race.

Competitors have always existed in NASCAR, but competition had never reached the boiling point that was achieved between the two sports drink brands in 2004.

As part of POWERade's deal with NASCAR, on most NASCAR tracks big blowup POWERade bottles are placed on the top of the winning driver's car. The idea is to give POWERade media exposure to go along with the celebration. However, Gatorade expected its drivers to emerge from their cars and trump POWERade by taking a swig of Gatorade in front of the cameras. The drivers, realizing that their marketing deals would be compromised if they didn't take care of Gatorade, did all they could to block the competition. Eventually it got to a point where some drivers were knocking the POWERade bottles off their cars when they won.

NASCAR driver Jimmie Johnson celebrated winning the New England 300 in July 2003 by opening a Gatorade in victory lane. Gatorade and its competitor POWERade both have a heavy presence in the sport. *(Rusty Jarrett/Getty Images)*

Even after NASCAR decried the practice, drivers had a tough time finding a resolution. Then things got even more complicated. When Jimmie Johnson won a race at the Pocono Raceway in June 2004, he was fined $10,000 for covering up the POWERade bottles with a cardboard sign. Although NASCAR officials were hoping that Gatorade and POWERade could peacefully coexist, no change in policy could result in one of the brands reluctantly leaving the sport in the near future.

Those who worked on the Gatorade brand feel that the competitive atmosphere made the brand stronger.

"We became a fine-tuned organization when Coke and Pepsi came at us," said Williams, who left Quaker in 1998 after a 28-year tenure. "We lived in fear of them for many years, but the competition became part of us. It made us focus, made us make changes, and made us accept our weaknesses and leverage our strengths."

Has POWERade's growth been slowed? Can Coca-Cola officials continue to position the brand differently and eat up more of Gatorade's market?

Oza, who left Coca-Cola to join Glaceau Vitamin Water in 2003, says he thinks Coca-Cola can still make headway against Gatorade.

"I think POWERade is a very credible competitor," Oza said. "If they do the right things in this long-term rivalry, they can get as much as 30 percent of the U.S. market."

Even if POWERade takes a greater chunk, Gatorade inventor Dr. Robert Cade says that he knows his invention will never be beaten at the top of the list.

"It was Napoleon who said that the army that hits 'the firstest with the mostest' is going to win," Cade said. "That's what happened with Gatorade. It was the firstest and no copies will ever defeat it."[17]

CHAPTER 8

The Gatorade Rules

WHEN QUAKER bought Stokely-Van Camp in 1983 for $220 million, many analysts thought that it had overpaid. The funny-looking and weird-tasting Gatorade was Stokely-Van Camp's major asset, and the year before it had netted only $90 million in business—0.1 percent of the U.S. beverage business at the time.[1] Although Gatorade owned 97 percent of the sports drink market, sales growth had been static for a number of years.

"To get in a bidding war for a mediocre company like Stokely is ridiculous,"[2] William Leach, a food analyst with Donaldson, Lufkin and Jenrette, said at the time.

After selling off everything but Pork & Beans and Gatorade, the net price of the acquisition was $95 million. By 1989, Gatorade's profits were $125 million, accounting for a fifth of Quaker's total profits.

Business Week called the deal one of the best acquisitions of the 1980s, and Leach, in 2002, was quick to call Gatorade's market share "almost illegal."[3] In the 18 years of Quaker's ownership, as the sports drink market grew by leaps and bounds, Gatorade remained the most dominant brand in its category in the United States.

This wasn't achieved by moments of luck. It was accomplished through a targeted and clear market strategy that was refined over and over again by people who understood what made the brand tick.

Although Quaker wasn't a beverage company, its executives knew how to deal with Gatorade. They used the same principles that had made the company's oatmeal and Aunt Jemima brands so successful.

"Within two years of having control of Gatorade, people who watched sports would have told you that it was among the top two or three brands that they associated with sporting events, and we were spending about one-tenth of what Budweiser and Miller were spending," Marineau said.

The following are nine business principles that helped Gatorade become one of the most powerful brands in modern-day business history. Many of these tenets are shared by other global leaders who have used and perfected them. It wasn't that the people at Quaker always knew what to do; often mistakes were made, and those managing the brand realized that these rules were key to remaining a leader in the marketplace.

1. Make Sure Your Product, Service, or Brand Is Unique and Know What Makes It Unique

When Quaker executives looked closely at what Stokely-Van Camp was doing with Gatorade, they noticed that the company was clearly a smaller corporation that was willing to do anything for a sale.

Since more than 25 percent of Gatorade's sales came during the summer months and the product was mostly selling in the southeast, Stokely-Van Camp was tempted to stray away from its core in order to boost profits. The company even tried heating up Gatorade and putting cinnamon sticks in it in order to try to sell it during the winter at ski slopes.

The drink started out as being sold only to athletic teams, but once Stokely realized that Gatorade could appeal to the mass market, it almost stopped positioning it as a sports drink. Stokely spent a lot of time and energy trying to increase awareness of the brand through advertising that didn't always include active athletes. When it did feature Gatorade's role as a thirst quencher, Stokely claimed that it moved through the body at a speed 12 times faster than water.

As soon as Quaker Oats acquired the Gatorade brand, executives knew that they had to find out what they had really purchased. By doing so, they could determine how effective the drink was and what audience they should sell it to.

Karen Hunter, an attorney who had been with Quaker since 1976, had also earned a bachelor of science in chemistry.

"I wanted to look at the product and make sure that it was really what they said it was," Hunter said. "The chairman [of Quaker Oats], Bill Smithburg—who drank it and lived it and breathed it— thought it was a wonderful product, but I was worried that we could have been sold swampwater."

"This is and was a very ethical company, and we lived by that in our oatmeal research in that we waited twenty years before we made the claims about its relationship to cholesterol," Hunter said. "We wanted to make sure that Quaker's equity wasn't harmed by things that were said about Gatorade that weren't true."

Quaker Oats executive Phil Marineau ordered that Gatorade be taken to a lab to find out its exact qualities. If it didn't travel through the body at a speed faster than water, he wanted to know it.

"When they told me they had the results, I thought I was going to have a heart attack," Marineau said.

Luckily, the scientists said that Gatorade did work—though it worked as fast as water, not 12 times faster as originally advertised.[4] The equal speed was sufficient because Gatorade had carbohydrates in it and would provide energy that water didn't.

"When I heard that, I knew that we had the ammunition to win," Marineau said. "It sounds small, but if it weren't for the test results that said what it did, we wouldn't be here."

It wasn't good enough that the properties of Gatorade were validated. Marineau realized that in order for the brand to stay on top, Quaker would have to constantly prove that it was the best thirst-quenching product in the world at all times. In 1985, Quaker started doing research and funding studies, with the goal of being the most knowledgeable organization in the world on the science of fluid replacement and sports nutrition. Three years later, the company opened the Gatorade Sports Science Institute (GSSI), complete with a lab in Barrington, Illinois, to make sure that the product did what it was supposed to do.

"What I was concerned about was that somebody was going to out-Gatorade Gatorade," said Marineau, who, while still at Quaker, took a position on the board of the American College of Sports Medicine. "Our goal was to use our relationships with researchers to stay ahead of the curve on the latest in thirst science."

This was done in much the same way that Henry Parsons Crowell, the founder of Quaker Oats, laid out his rules of conduct for the company. In his code, he wrote that the goal was to make the best oatmeal: "No matter what the cost, make changes when quality can be improved."[5]

Gatorade officials say that the formula has been virtually untouched because the original formulation was very sound, but that does not diminish the capital that the brand allocates to GSSI. When a competitor has touted a new ingredient that Gatorade doesn't have, GSSI has responded with clinical data showing why the company didn't put that ingredient in Gatorade.

"We say that unless it's peer reviewed, unless you can prove it, we're not putting it in our beverage," said Gatorade's sports marketing chief Tom Fox.

As more and more food and drink manufacturers have been adding the most popular supplement of the day to their products, the Gatorade brand has been very careful not to tinker with its formulation in order to ride the hip craze of the moment.

"One of our jobs for the company is to provide the scientific guidelines—studying what, if anything, we should do with our product as well as helping to develop new products," said Dr. Bob Murray, director of GSSI. "We have to keep our ear close to the ground with new ideas regarding ingredients. Our counsel over the years has been that there are all sorts of potential opportunities, but there are going to be very few real opportunities."

Although its Performance Series, which is directed at high-intensity athletes, has products that include vitamins A, C, and E, zinc, and protein, the Gatorade that the general consumer sees has never included the latest ingredients of the moment—such as creatine, chromium picolinate, ephedra, and taurine.

Gatorade might have been even more popular if its marketers had introduced a special Gatorade with a popular supplement in it, but by not doing that, they avoided risking exposure when that supplement was phased out for the next latest thing. Since Gatorade stands for the ultimate in sweat replenishment, its brand managers have to distinguish the fads from the future. With Quaker continuing to sponsor research on the science of sweat, odds are that the brand won't fall far behind if a new ingredient is needed in the marketplace.

2. Never Stop Researching the Marketplace

It's no secret that understanding the environment that surrounds a brand, its present and its future, is the key to building a long-term business. Gatorade would have ruined its mystique if Quaker Oats executives had continued to sell the beverage the way Stokely-Van Camp had been selling it. But the drink was saved because Quaker executives recognized—even under pressure to get returns from its acquisition—that the thirst-quenching market was going to be enough of a business to make the company profitable. So it steered the brand back on course to its original purpose.

"We saw the baby boomers really coming into their prime, and the whole notion of exercise and getting out there and running was going to be huge," Marineau said. "So we went back and looked at it and said, 'This really fits a niche, and there should be tremendous potential if we do this right.' And we took three months to study the market, to study the brand, and we came up with five key strategies that even to this day drive the business."

Those strategies are (1) own thirst-quenching benefit, (2) drive availability to the point of thirst, (3) drive flavor and package pro-liferation, (4) be on the sidelines from kid to pro, and (5) be the most knowledgeable organization in the science of fluid replace-ment in the world.

Had the exercise boom not been anticipated or had it been ana-
lyzed as a momentary blip, Gatorade could have lost the advantage of dominating the category by straying into another sector
of the marketplace.

Gatorade was fortunate to have been purchased by Quaker Oats.
If the brand had been purchased by a soft drink company, it is not
likely that it would have been the innovator that it in fact became.
This is because Quaker Oats was always devoted to research. In 1956,
it opened the John Stuart Research Laboratories in Barrington,
Illinois. This lab is the home of all product, process, and packaging
research for Quaker's foods and beverages. Under its roof are more
than 250 employees who specialize in cereal science, flavor chemistry, beverage processing, and packaging technology, among other
areas of expertise.

Just because Gatorade was still dominating the market in the late
1990s didn't mean that the executives managing the brand sat on
their hands and gave themselves credit for controlling the marketplace. Instead, they reinvested some of their profits in research to
better understand who their current consumers were and why they
bought the product.

In the late 1990s, Gatorade brand managers commissioned a
consumer-segmentation study. The study included the opinions of
thousands of people, with the goal of trying to understand their
behaviors regarding physical activity and their choice of beverage
while they were active.

They discovered that there were several active segments in the
United States. Each one was motivated to exercise by a different factor—one group did it for the love of sports and competition, another
group did it for the exercise, while another group was active because
of their jobs.

The goal of the study was to find out about each group and how many beverages its members consumed. Did one group drink more than another? What groups were maxing out their volume and what groups might need more Gatorade? Research revealed that the greatest volume and the greatest growth potential resided with those playing team sports.

"They wanted to kick the other guy's butt, and that knowledge helped shape the focus of a lot of the marketing communication," said Cindy Alston, Gatorade's vice president of equity development.

The immediate result of the research was Gatorade's "Is It In You?" slogan—a slogan that was meant to speak to the active competitor. The line was a double entendre that was asking consumers if they had the will in them to battle on the playing field and then if they had the product in them. The double meaning was driven home further by the athletes in the commercial sweating the color of Gatorade's flavors. It was a natural, since those who worked on the brand were always said to bleed green, much like Federal Express employees are said to bleed purple.

"When we overlaid that colored sweat—Gatorade is pouring through this guy, and he's succeeding and working hard and replacing what he is losing—what we found is that with that technique and tagline, our emotion equity scores went up," said John Frazer, executive vice president of business strategy for Gatorade's advertising firm, Element 79 Partners. The slogan has been so effective that Gatorade has used it continuously since 1999.

"Our core group of consumers consists of the competitors—the people who are all about winning," said current Gatorade president Chuck Maniscalco, who started working with Quaker brands in 1980. "But of that group that works out five times a week, they only drink Gatorade an average of once a week. So we think there's an enormous opportunity to tap into that. We're smart enough to know that we need to start looking harder at the hot and sweaty occasions and how we penetrate those occasions."

Another study was commissioned to try to determine the reasons why consumers were particularly loyal to Gatorade. While many companies could identify a straightforward reason why a majority of their customers liked their brand, this equity study showed that the channels to a loyal Gatorade consumer were quite complicated. Some were loyal because they had used Gatorade as a child, another group was loyal because Gatorade worked when they needed it, some used Gatorade because they supported a particular sport or were interested in a particular athlete, while others said they loved Gatorade because the pros used it. The differing routes to loyalty proved to those running Gatorade that they had to continue to support all their programs, from grassroots to pros, because they were all valid points of entry into gaining new consumers of the product.

"I'm not sure that the consumer has changed all that much over the last 15 years," Alston said. "But our knowledge of the consumer has changed, and therefore we have the ability to create programs that really connect with them . . . . Part of driving brand loyalty is talking to a consumer in a way that shows that we understand them and what motives them to play and the rewards they get from playing sports. A lot of those everyman athletes really say, 'This brand gets me; I can embrace it, and I can use it when I play sports because they really know why I play and they can help me when I play.' That's a deeper message then what you get from a celebrity athlete."

Gatorade has become a very successful brand because of this constant research and awareness of the marketplace. It's easy to be constantly motivated when a company is a market follower, but leaders have to continue to push themselves every day to make sure they never stop innovating and never become satisfied.

How have Gatorade executives managed to stay on top of the game even after dominating it for nearly four decades? They have changed their definition of what the marketplace is. Instead of thinking of their market share as 80 to 90 percent of the sports drink category, they put Gatorade in the multibillion-dollar "active thirst market." When Gatorade was seen as competing with water and soda, all of a sudden it had only a 10 percent share of the market, or 10 billion of 100 billion quarts of nonalcoholic beverages consumed in the United States.

In 2000, Sue Wellington went public by saying that she wouldn't rest until tap water was used only for washing dishes and taking showers.

"If we couldn't keep inventing this point of sweat opportunity and started looking in the rearview mirror and just trying to steal share amongst the sports drink companies, we would have gone backwards," Wellington said.

Of course, the irony of it all is that today both Pepsi and Coca-Cola are doing pretty well selling purified bottled tap water with their Aquafina and Dasani brands. They are the No. 1 and No. 2 bottled water brands in the United States.

"We don't do this [look at Gatorade as having 10 percent of the active market] to make the investment community feel better," Maniscalco said. "We do it because nine times out of ten, people who are hot and sweaty are drinking the wrong stuff."

"We will spend a hundred times more energy trying to figure out how we can continue to fulfill consumers' needs with the active thirst category than on anything else," said Tom Fox. "Quite honestly, there's such a big gap between us and number two that we've got to keep our eye on the real opportunity."

3. Identify Drivers of the Business and Take Care of Them

If there are any two people who deserve great credit for defining Gatorade's strategy, it's Phil Marineau and Bill Schmidt. Schmidt was the bronze medalist in the javelin in the 1972 Olympics and competed in the 1976 and 1980 games.

It was Schmidt's experience as an athlete at the highest level that allowed him to understand who the drivers of the Gatorade business were going to be.

Too often, organizations aim to sell directly to consumers, but don't reach the influencers who help initiate those sales. When Schmidt took over Gatorade's sports marketing in September of 1983, he knew exactly who the brand influencers were.

At the time, it was Gatorade's aim to make sure that it was on the field of play. Gatorade had relationships with the professional organizations, but those relationships were essentially just league licenses—individual teams could do what they wished as far as what sports drink they used.

Stokely had started to establish some relationships with the team trainers, but Schmidt realized that if he could develop a good rapport with the trainers, he'd have a better chance at getting Gatorade on the sidelines.

"They were the gatekeepers," Schmidt said. "They were the ones who decided what to give the athletes, and they were the ones who were going to put it on the field of play."

Schmidt realized that up until that point, trainers had been mostly ignored by the teams. So his strategy was to take care of them so that they would take care of Gatorade.

Trainers were very loosely organized at the time, so Schmidt started to support them, fund them, and provide them with a mission

t. He hired a small public relations firm to manage their account and developed a phone directory for the NFL trainers. With Marineau's blessing, he gave them a stipend of $20,000. A decade later, the NFL Trainers Association was making five times that amount, and when a trainer was fired, he received a lump-sum check that was provided thanks to the Gatorade money.

Schmidt wasn't buying the relationship. He was merely taking care of the trainers, providing them with the services that they needed. Allocating dollars to organize trainers was not directly in the line of sales. It probably didn't look great on the books, but it was viewed as essential.

"The relationship was born out of something that was real," said longtime Gatorade attorney Karen Hunter. "Gatorade was already on the sidelines. The athletic trainers were buying it and placing it there because they knew it worked. But the trainers were responsible for the care of the whole athlete. They knew we were about science, so they were coming to us for help, for information. What we saw was a need. They needed to speak to each other and to speak as a cohesive voice. That could only help the trainers gain credibility. Thus, the idea of an association of trainers was born, and we simply helped fund its creation."

Not only did trainers help to place Gatorade on the sidelines in the right places, but they also were Schmidt's eyes and ears at the point of attack. If competition was entering the marketplace, Schmidt would hear about it first through the trainers.

When it was holiday time, all the trainers got something from Gatorade. Schmidt had a $40,000 budget for Christmas gifts.

"It wasn't lavish spending," Schmidt said. "It was prudent, direct, and targeted. And it was a way to make people feel tied to us, particularly when we weren't directly paying them anything."

The trainers would receive a notebook with a Gatorade logo on it or a package of Quaker products. Schmidt would send them business-card holders, portfolios, and pens. Schmidt would also send gifts to the marketing people and to the owners of the teams. One year, NFL owners got a humidor with a Gatorade logo on it. And, yes, it came full of cigars.

Simply put, the trainers were the point of attack.

"We never asked for anything when we gave this to them," Schmidt said. "It was just understood. The thing that would come out of most of the meetings with the trainers was, 'What else can we do for you? How else could we help?'"

Quaker's commitment to this group of influencers has paid off.

"I was having breakfast with the strength and conditioning coach of the University of Kentucky football team and he was telling me about his job," said Chuck Maniscalco. "He said he had a certain amount to spend on beverages, supplements, and food. So I asked him, 'How much of that budget do you spend on Gatorade?' And he told me about 80 percent of those dollars. I asked him, 'Why so much?' And he said, 'Because I trust you.' This speaks volumes to what we have become as leaders of this business. We have bred a level of trust where our consumers believe that we will do the right thing, and that is something that we value, cherish, and respect."

Ever notice how perfectly the Gatorade is placed on the sidelines? Schmidt and current sports marketing head Tom Fox do not provide schematics showing the trainers how to display the Gatorade in areas where it can be seen. The trainers simply do it because of the relationships they have with the brand. They place Gatorade in key exposure spots, such as lining up cups above the bench where the cameras will always focus on them. They call

Schmidt or Fox and say, "Hey, did you see that?" Building relationships with the drivers pays off.

Bill Schmidt identified the trainers as people who would influence both the perception and the placement of his product. Other Gatorade executives realized that having the right product in the hands of the hard-core athlete, another influencer, was also important.

Sometimes that product wasn't the Gatorade that you could buy at the stores. And sometimes that product wasn't something that Gatorade made or could make a profit on. But the company made the product anyway because Gatorade was created for athletes, and it wanted the brand to mean something to every type of athlete, especially the opinion leaders.

That's one of the reasons why Gatorade created the Performance Series, a line of products most of which the everyday consumer will never see on the shelves, although they are available on the brand's web site. As part of the line, Gatorade has the Endurance Formula (which is now available in supermarkets nationwide), a Gatorade that has more sodium and potassium in it, as well as additional calcium and magnesium. It is geared to athletes who are working out harder for a longer period of time. Gatorade also produces a high-carbohydrate energy drink, which at 310 calories would not be a big seller in stores. In NBA and NFL locker rooms, you'll find Gatorade chocolate, vanilla, and strawberry nutrition shakes, with 370 calories, 8 grams of fat, and 20 grams of protein in each can.

"To the degree that you don't do a Gatorade energy drink to service the pro athletes because you don't think it's a commercial opportunity, that's not good," said Sue Wellington. "It means that you are not taking care of your bread and butter."

It also means that hard-core athletes are forced to leave your brand family if they want to get a more serious sports beverage, and

Gatorade certainly didn't want to have sponsorship deals with players who, when the cameras were off, were using something else.

Wellington said that each year Gatorade would allocate about $7 million for servicing the athletes and making sure that they had products that connected to them. This might not have made sense from a financial standpoint because of the lack of ability to bring these products to the marketplace, but it was done.

"There were times where a new executive would come in and question the dollars we allocated here, and you'd say, 'Leave it alone,' and throw yourself in front of it," Wellington said. "Because if they stop doing stuff like that, that's when a business crashes. As the business grows, they are going to have to allocate more dollars in this area."

At times, Gatorade has tried to make commercial opportunities out of this. Several times, it has tried to release a high-carbohydrate energy drink, once in the early 1980s under the name Gatorlode 280 (the number of calories in the drink), and most recently under the name TORQ. One of the difficulties is that it's difficult to convince people to take in that many calories through a liquid if they are not running marathons. The other issue, particularly with TORQ, was that consumers compared it to the Red Bulls and Rockstars of the world, when it was actually a different type of energy drink.

"If you talk to the serious athlete, they know that Nike is out there working very hard to try to find that next piece of technology that is going to make them run better, run faster, swim faster, play better golf, all of those things," said Tom Fox. "We're exactly the same way. If you walk into an NFL locker room right now, you'll see a refrigerator full of Gatorade products that the consumer will never touch."

Only rarely has Gatorade held back from producing something because of the lack of commercial opportunity. At one point, a

Gatorade "goo" product called Reload, a predecessor of today's PowerGel, was produced, but it was eventually nixed because of lack of commercial opportunity.

Just as executives for the brand try to stay ahead of trends for the sake of everyday Gatorade, they devote time and money to making sure that the next generation of athletes is using a Gatorade-branded product.

Most recently, elite football players at the University of Oklahoma have been cooperating with GSSI to learn more about how the elite athlete's body works. Dr. Randy Eichner, the team's internist, is on the GSSI Sports Medicine Review Board.

In 2002, the researchers used sweat patches to find out specifics relating to the contents of a player's sweat. It was discovered through this study that those players who cramp up were losing about twice as much sodium and fluid as the other players.

In 2003, players took a radio-transmitting pill designed by NASA to find out if there was a relationship between cramping and body temperature—and to help figure out why players cramp and get heatstroke. In 2004, GSSI did tests on players to see if they lose muscle, along with water and fat, while playing.

Gatorade was invented at a time when 30 to 40 athletes a year were dying from heatstroke. While that number had declined to an average of about two athletes per year by 2004, Gatorade officials say that GSSI strives to help athletes optimize their performance through research and education in hydration and nutrition science.

4. Never Stop Working to Get Your Next Consumer

From the time of Quaker Oats's acquisition of Gatorade, executives working on the brand had always understood the value of grassroots marketing. Putting the product on the NFL sidelines for the pros to drink and consumers to see was great for the brand, and advertising with a catchy jingle added to the mix. But it was always important to spend money to reinvest in the consumers, making sure that Gatorade was sponsoring amateur events and was available at a place where active athletes were thirsty.

"If we're only there for the pros because they are on TV, and we're not there for the young kid—seven or eight years old—and the young tennis player who starts to feel that serve pop, who starts to get his timing down and starts to feel like he may be able to play the sport, then we are not a leader," said Tom Fox, who in January 2005 was named No. 32 on the *Sporting News's* Power 100, a list that tracks the most powerful people in sports.

In 1985, Gatorade started to develop a meaningful relationship with the kid athlete community. In order to get the product into the hands of the right people, brand managers felt that they had to identify which sports most people participated in and which sports most people watched.

Together with Bruce Weber, the publisher of *Scholastic Coach and Athletic Director* magazine, marketer Bill Schmidt came up with a list of those sports—football, baseball, basketball, running, and soccer.

These were the sports that the company was going to spend the most time and money on. Over the years, it perfected the growing of its next generation of consumers.

When the sponsor dollars became available, many organizations obviously wanted to have Gatorade pitch in, but executives knew that they couldn't possibly sponsor every Pop Warner football league and every Little League Baseball group.

So Gatorade developed a screening process for brand managers to determine whether it made sense to make a deal. This process has gotten more rigorous over the years. Some of the questions include: Does this fall within our identified core sports? Does this event know how to give the participants a quality Gatorade experience? Do the organizers plan on using Gatorade, or do they just want us for the goody bag? (The latter answer means no sponsorship.) Are the organizers willing to teach kids about the importance of hydration, or are they just going to fill our orange coolers with water?

If the alliance works, things pay off.

Said Alston: "If you are a little, young athlete and you start playing sports and drinking Gatorade, you are significantly more likely to be loyal to Gatorade your entire active life."

Just as the bottom line didn't make sense when Gatorade developed products for the hard-core athletes, the bottom line didn't make sense when Gatorade started giving out awards to elite high school athletes. But there has still been a payoff.

At the same time that Schmidt was working with Bruce Weber to determine the best sports to drive product to young athletes, he also decided that Gatorade should reach out to the young athlete community.

Schmidt had the idea of getting in touch with every high school federation in all 50 states and the District of Columbia. With help from around the country, Gatorade would give Circle of Champions awards in seven sports in every state. The awards would be based not only on on-the-field prowess, but on academics as well. This would show that Gatorade wasn't just hoping to pluck young customers, it would also recognize the best of what those customers did. It also helped Gatorade associate with excellence—as many of the winners, not surprisingly, went on to become the best pros.

In 1986, the national football award went to a young man named Emmitt Smith, who of course went on to be the NFL's leading rusher. Other award winners of note include Ken Griffey Jr., Shaquille

O'Neal, Peyton Manning, Marion Jones, Vince Carter, Derek Jeter, and Chamique Holdsclaw.

"It was our way of giving back and reinforcing where our heart and soul was," said P. J. Sinopoli, who was with Gatorade from 1983 to 2002 and traveled around the country handing out the awards. "Almost to a one this was the biggest accolade they had received in their athletic careers. The payoff was not so much the marketing of it. We spent way more money on this program than the exposure we would get from a traditional commercial."

Another group that Gatorade managers were determined to reach was Hispanics. The Hispanic beverage market reached about $25 billion in 2003, but Gatorade began advertising to Hispanic people in the late 1980s. Research had shown that Hispanics were more brand loyal than most consumers. When Gatorade got into the marketplace, it found this to be true—not only were Hispanics drinking a disproportionate amount of beverages, but they were drinking a higher amount of Gatorade than Caucasians. In 1996, Gatorade unveiled ¡Mandarina!, which had excellent results in test markets in south Florida, south Texas, and southern California.

"By the time companies started getting to the Latino market, after the results of the 2000 census, we had been talking to them in their language for a decade," said Gatorade spokesman Andy Horrow.

Gatorade didn't just translate its advertising into Spanish. The company hired Latino-specific ad agencies (Berry Brown/Grupo Quatro and Dieste Harmel Partners) that were responsible for writing, creating, and producing their own ads based on the brand strategy. Gatorade also committed itself to developing a whole line of flavors for Latinos. In 2001, it unveiled the Xtremo subline—Mango Electrico, Citrico Vibrante, and Tropical Intenso—with bilingual labels.

Like the advertising strategy, the choice of flavors is also tailored to the ethnicity. Although it is not common in the United States, the mango is the most popular fruit to eat in the world.

The Xtremo subline was unveiled throughout the United States, and mango became one of the brand's most popular flavors. This shouldn't have been a surprise. In January 2003, the U.S. Hispanic population had risen to 37 million. Hispanics were now the largest minority in America, surpassing African Americans for the first time ever. Gatorade was once again ahead of the curve.

One key to interesting the next consumer in the product is that brand managers don't forget the core market. Gatorade was successful at achieving that balance.

5. Packaging Counts

The beverage market has always used changes in packaging to drive sales. Coke realized the greater selling potential with the six-pack— then called the "six box"—in 1923 and the 26-ounce family size in 1935. Pepsi became more of a premium brand thanks to the swirled glass bottle that the company rolled out in 1958.

But it was actually Quaker Oats that is credited for being the first company to recognize packaging as a sales vehicle instead of seeing it solely as a distribution vehicle. The company differentiated itself by packaging its oats in attractive, colorful boxes on the shelves. Prior to that, oatmeal was sold from a barrel that was set on the floor of the grocery store. The sack of oats was often left open, and it was unsanitary.

Early Gatorade research found that consumers were more package loyal than brand loyal. A look in their refrigerators would reveal may products with the same type of packaging. Therefore, Gatorade's goal was to vary the type of packaging in order to have a better chance of getting into the consumer's hands.

In the early 1980s, the only sizes that were available were 32- and 46-ounce glass bottles. These sizes weren't particularly appropriate because each bottle had two to six servings in it, depending on how the servings were counted. It was important to get smaller.

When Gatorade was purchased by Quaker Oats, Coca-Cola's motto was "Within an arm's reach of desire." Quaker Oats execs used this motto internally to remind themselves that they wanted to get their product to all the points of sweat. When Gatorade was introduced in a single-serving 16-ounce bottle, sales took off.

Quaker Oats also pioneered the invention of the hot-fill PET (polyethylene terephthalate) plastic bottles. Gatorade is not made like a soft drink. It uses a hot-fill process. That means that its bottles have to be filled while hot in order to sterilize the internal surface of the container. Prior to Gatorade's innovation, getting plastic not to warp when the bottle cooled down was a significant obstacle.

When Gatorade changed its 32-ounce bottle from glass to plastic, sales volume increased by 25 percent in the first year alone. Company officials believe that the change in materials drove sales for the entire brand up by 7 percent.

"That was more powerful than having Michael Jordan," Marineau said. "Having that brand in plastic was absolutely huge, because now mom could take it to the soccer game, you could take it to Little League games. It allowed you to get on every sideline for every activity known to man, which was our goal. You could carry it everywhere, and you didn't have to worry about carrying glass or breaking it and having some kid get hurt."

Gatorade went to a wide-mouth bottle that made it easier to gulp during exercise or a game. Then, in February 1995, it was the first brand to put a noncarbonated drink in a push-pull squeezable sports bottle.

"There was a lot of hand-wringing because it required a lot of capital," said Barry Judge, a Gatorade marketer who convinced those managing the brand that the innovation was worth the investment. "When we did our focus groups, the kids wouldn't let go of it."

Within three years, one-quarter of all of Gatorade's retail sales were from drinks sold in its sports bottles.

Over time, changes in packaging got significantly more scientific and complex. The brand hired Metaphase Design Group, an ergonomic product designer, to design its ergonomic sports bottle called EDGE (ergonomically designed Gatorade experience). The company visited sporting events, studied how big the human mouth was, studied whether athletes preferred to squeeze or suck, and molded casts of athletes' hands and fingers.

The result was a bottle that provided an easier drinking experience. It was introduced in March 2000, and consumers responded with double-digit growth in some regions of the country. The knob on top of the bottle turns to open, making it possible to open and close it with the mouth. The design won the Package of the Year Award from the publication *Food & Drug Packaging*.

"Over 20 years, you could see us get closer to where people sweat—in schools and work sites where we hadn't always used to be," said longtime Gatorade executive Sue Wellington. "The packaging had a lot to do with that."

Pressured by POWERade's smaller packaging and the growth of Procter & Gamble's Sunny Delight, Gatorade knew that it had to use smaller packaging for Tweens (kids between the ages of 8 and 12). Sunny Delight was being advertised to mothers and children as an after-exercise/play drink. Gatorade reacted by introducing a subline called All-Stars, a product for Tweens. The company made different flavors, like Pink Lemonade, but it was essentially the brand's foray into 12-ounce bottles. Not only was the 20-ounce Gatorade probably too large to get on the field of play for the young kid, but the smaller bottles were also a lot more affordable to buy in bulk.

By the time the folks at Procter & Gamble took things a step further by extending the orange juice brand to a sports drink called Sunny D Intense Sport, Gatorade was already in the marketplace. Another competitor in the child hydration market is Capri Sun, which has sought to differentiate itself through pouches that contain less than seven ounces of fluid.

While getting smaller was important to Gatorade, so was getting bigger. In March 2003, Gatorade introduced its biggest ready-to-drink package ever: its rectangular plastic gallon bottle. This bottle is intended to be economical for large groups. Since the bottle weighs eight pounds, there is a bail handle near the top of the cap for easy carrying. Hand grips on the bottle also make the bottle easier to pour from.

6. Learn from Your Mistakes

One of Gatorade's greatest mistakes was Gatorade Light. In the late 1980s and early 1990s, the low-calorie business was taking off. Even Häagen-Dazs, of all premium brands, had relented by coming out with frozen yogurt. So Gatorade tried to bring women—who made up only about 20 percent of its customers—into the franchise by creating Gatorade Light. The drink had exactly half the calories that Gatorade had and less sodium.

Gatorade Light was introduced on February 20, 1990.

"Back then you were big and bad; you needed everything in Gatorade," said a voice-over in the ad, with black-and-white high school–type highlights. "But times have changed." The screen flashed to color featuring fuller-figured, older athletes. "You're still big and bad. We just don't want to see you get too big."[6]

In order to lower the calories, Quaker had to use saccharin as a sweetener, which hurt the taste of the product. But the larger issue with the product was that brand managers realized that consumers wanted a full Gatorade or nothing.

"Women, on average, do not want to put stuff back when they exercise," said Peter Vitulli, who was overseeing U.S. Gatorade at the time of Gatorade Light. "They want to lose that weight. We learned that when we put it in test markets. It wasn't a disaster; it was just a learning experience."

The other issue was alienating their core users, who, much as Coke drinkers asked what was wrong with the classic Coke when New Coke came out in 1985, were asking why they were drinking Gatorade when Gatorade Light was indirectly telling them that they didn't need to put back the calories. Gatorade Light was quickly phased out.

Gatorade executives eventually identified what they were really trying to create—a product connected to Gatorade, but with a different brand name and a completely different formulation. Gatorade executives learned from Gatorade Light that Gatorade wasn't halfway anything—it was a hard-core, all-out brand. But those managing the brand knew that they were onto something with the light consumer. Gatorade rejecters weren't brand rejecters. They just didn't want to drink Gatorade.

"I really want to be part of the Nike brand, but I'm always forced to accept another brand because Nikes just don't fit my feet well," said Sue Wellington. "It was sort of that way with committed exercisers. They really respected us and wanted to be part of the Gatorade brand, but it wasn't for them."

The eventual result of learning from the Gatorade Light mistake was the creation of Propel, Gatorade's flavored water, which launched regionally in 2000. The water has vitamins B, C, and E in it and has only ten calories per serving. Through good taste, it encourages those who work out to stay hydrated, but not at the expense of ruining their workout by putting the calories back into their bodies. In the first nine months of 2004, Propel's business grew by 48.7 percent, and the product is the market leader in flavored fitness water, which makes up 10 percent of U.S. water sales.[7]

One of the reasons why Quaker grew the business so well is that the company wasn't scared to move away from the three main flavors—lemon-lime, orange, and fruit punch. Through differentiation, the company found new customers.

In 1997, Gatorade introduced national sublines. It started with Frost—a lighter-tasting line with vague names such as Whitewater Splash, Alpine Snow, and Glacier Freeze. In 2003, under Pepsi's management, Gatorade unveiled the X-Factor line, the mixing of two Gatorade flavors in one bottle.

Gatorade now has almost 50 flavors worldwide and there are virtually no natural fruit flavors left. But those managing the brand are extra careful when dreaming up new flavors, an art that is getting increasingly tougher over time.

The nightmare of Midnight Thunder is fresh in their minds. The flavor, which was introduced in April 1998, was unveiled because it was thought that teens would love it. The color of the drink was black, and the flavor was blackberry. But while it was meant to be cool, contemporary, and edgy, it just didn't work.

"It was a pretty big bust," Wellington said. "When it came down to it, black Gatorade is kind of hard to reason your way through. If you are in an athletic moment, reaching for a black liquid probably isn't at the top of your list. It was trying to be too sexy and forgot that we're a sports drink."

7. Seek to Connect Emotion and Passion to the Brand

A brand is only as good as the people who are behind it. Gatorade didn't fight off the onslaught of Pepsi (All Sport) and Coke (POWERade) in the early 1990s by simply having a good product. They also had good people who didn't want to lose.

"When Coke and Pepsi first came in, our whole team, our organization, felt very defeated," said former Quaker Oats marketer Peggy Dyer. "At first it was like, 'Oh, the big beverage boys are coming in; how can we possibly win?' And then it was, 'No. We are going to win. We are the A team. They are not going to put their A team on that business, and we can win.' And it was really the confidence of the whole of the organization that we could in fact win."

Many people at Gatorade became the brand—they lived it and they breathed it.

"The people are almost inseparable from the product and product personality," Wellington said. "It was always that way. And I think if there ever was a time that we lost our way, it was because the combination of the people who were working on the business didn't have the same passion for sport and passion for winning and passion for the elixir. You could feel that competitive atmosphere in the hallways back to when Quaker Oats bought it."

Throughout the mid-1980s, Bill Schmidt gave himself a goal of making sure that every NFL team used Gatorade. He did an incredible job, securing as many teams as possible in a decade's time. But he was always being pushed by others within the company until he had the entire league. (Now the league grants automatic exclusivity.) So when the San Francisco 49ers appeared on the field in 1989 with a new product called Powerburst, executives who saw their games would constantly remind Schmidt to make sure it was a Gatorade team the following year. It almost happened that way by default. Powerburst was made for the team by a company that was partly owned by then-49ers owner Eddie DeBartolo Jr. But since its main carbohydrate was fructose, many athletes who drank a lot of it got upset stomachs. That combined with Gatorade's dominance was the death knell for the brand.

Of course, it's easier to have emotion and passion for a brand that is a market leader.

"Gatorade is considered a plum account, and everyone wants to work on it," said Danny Schuman of Element 79, which also does advertising for mostly PepsiCo brands. "So not only is there competition to be involved with Gatorade, there's competition for the people who work on it to do better work."

Said Gatorade's current president, Chuck Maniscalco:

For the people who work on Gatorade, this isn't just a business. The brand is part of their DNA, their heart, and their soul. How people who work on Gatorade feel is not something that can be written on a piece of paper. Their personal insights and passion are like nothing I've ever seen—from the depth of our understanding of consumers, the depth of understanding athletes, the depth of understanding influencers, and the depth of understanding the brand. It leads us to have an intensity and depth of debate that I've never seen in my career.

Those who feel so strongly about the brand they work for have also done a good job of eliciting feelings of passion and emotion from the consumer. For every helping of outrageous ads devised to break through the clutter, there are usually a couple of ads that reach consumers because they are real and poignant. Gatorade, much like Nike, has made a living out of touching, relevant advertising.

The "Is It In You?" campaign is an example of this. Armed with data, Gatorade wanted to tap into the active, competitive team-sports athletes to get them to think more about drinking the product. The company provided both the functional physical message and the emotional one in the double meaning of the slogan.

One of Gatorade's most popular ads was an emotional spot called "Love Hurts," which ran in 1997. Amazingly, up until that time, all of Gatorade's ads had featured athletes in positive moments—baskets and goals were scored and pitches were hit.

But in 1996, Nike ran an ad during the Summer Olympics in which athletes are trying their best—a boxer gets bloodied, a runner throws up.

"We showed it [the Nike ad] to Gatorade users in focus groups because part of how we learn how to do things is not only talking to consumers about our own stuff, but also showing them other things that are happening in the world of sports that we think are interesting and seeing what we can discern from them," Alston said.

While many consumers thought that Nike went too far with the spot, which was unofficially dubbed by many as "Just Spew It," Gatorade felt that it was a good message. The result was Gatorade's version, which was a little less graphic and had Nazareth's "Love Hurts" song in the background.

"When we showed that to athletes, they had smiles on their faces," said Schuman, one of the creative forces behind Gatorade's ad. "That is a really compelling and relevant insight to athletes. This is part of the game—I win, I lose. But the fact that it sometimes hurts doesn't deter me at all. It makes me love it even more."

One of the company's best emotional pieces of print advertising featured the Gatorade ingredients written on an IV bag in the same plain font that is usually used on IV bags. The bag, which this time was filled with orange liquid, suggested why Gatorade was better than the competition. It seemed to say that Gatorade was necessary and useful. Showing the solution in a nontraditional setting helped grab the attention of the reader.

Eye-popping commercials or advertisements often tap the emotions of those watching or reading, but they are not always rational.

In 1983, Quaker executives were being pressured by analysts who said that they had overpaid to acquire Stokely-Van Camp's assets. They therefore wanted to make a memorable television campaign for Gatorade for the 1984 Summer Olympics in Los Angeles.

One of the ads that they had produced was dubbed "Thirst Slayer."

The ad featured a cast of women charioteers and barbarian-type men competing as gladiators in a Roman coliseum. After they competed, they'd drink Gatorade. "Put away your beers, soft drinks, and wines; drink the one true beverage," the voice-over said. The ad ended with a screen that said "Gatorade. Thirst Slayer."

While the advertising was cute and memorable, focus groups admitted that it didn't motivate them to go out and buy a Gatorade. Perhaps it was much like Mean Joe Greene—while the spot might have been emotional, it didn't seem to make a rational association between the product and the consumer.

Cindy Alston knew that some of Gatorade's advertising must have resonated with the important core-athlete group when she stood at the 40th mile marker on the 120-mile bike ride along the lava fields of Kona for the 1994 Ironman.

The athletes cycling along were given a choice of Gatorade or water, and Alston felt proud of how many held out their hand for Gatorade instead of water.

"I remember listening to the athletes cycle by me at God knows what speed and ask for Gatorade in as many different dialects and accents as you can imagine," Alston said. "So it was Gatorade, GAY-to-rade, Gat-o-RADE. It was a moment I won't forget because we tried to convince people through television advertising to drink this stuff because it works, and there is no better testament than watching and experiencing this in the real world."

It is important to understand that even great brands can go off the path. The Gatorade commercial set to the words of Maya Angelou's poem "Still I Rise" was meant to convey emotion and passion.

The ad, which ran in 2000, had Angelou reading her own work, juxtaposed with scenes of athletes playing sports. Brand executives soon realized that the spot was too heady for sports, which are supposed to be visceral.

8. Stay Disciplined

With any major brand, the temptation is to use the brand name to branch out, but cannibalization of the brand is always a risk.

Before Quaker Oats acquired Gatorade, Stokely-Van Camp had licensed the Gatorade brand name for a gum called Gatorgum (its motto: "Thirst-quenching gum for active sports-minded people"). It was a long-term licensing deal that was passed around to a series of candy makers, including Fleer, Vicks, and Swell. The license was still in play in the late 1980s.

The problem with the gum was that it had no benefit that was similar to what Gatorade did for the body. Further hurting Quaker Oats was the fact that it wasn't a good seller.

"It was a dreadful product, and I thought it was terrible that the Gatorade trademark was associated with it in any way," Vitulli said. "So when the license ran out, we discontinued it."

But Quaker Oats executives made their own mistakes as well.

Shortly after Pepsi and Coca-Cola started telling the public that their drinks tasted better than Gatorade, Quaker brand managers relented. They unveiled a drink called Freestyle, a juice-based sports drink that would taste better than Gatorade. It didn't succeed.

In 1994, Gatorade introduced a drink called Sunbolt, characterized as a morning drink. It was advertised as the drink to help the "energy crisis" that people had in the mornings, and it was sold in the Northeast for six months. But the drink, while it sported the Gatorade logo, had none of the characteristics of a sports drink. It was high in carbohydrates and high in caffeine (the 12-ounce, 210-calorie drink had as much caffeine as a can of Coke). Sales weren't awful, but Gatorade executives felt that the disconnect with consumers made it hard to rationalize as a brand extension.

"When we took it off the market, there were a lot of consumer calls asking where it was," Sinopoli said. "It filled a niche for some people, but from an equity standpoint it was a dangerous direction to go in. It wasn't for the athlete, and it probably should have been managed under a separate brand name."

While current Gatorade executives say they are happy with the execution of Propel, some aren't so sure that this product doesn't hurt the value of the core brand, since it doesn't have the same benefits as Gatorade.

A firm connection between Gatorade and Propel was made in Propel's early advertising, with the slogan being "What if Gatorade Made Water?" But Gatorade is very careful not to mix and match the brands. Propel will never be on the sidelines of the NFL or in the dugout for a USA Softball game.

The most recent brand extension to have sputtered was Gatorade energy bars.

Quaker test marketed its energy bar entry—called Gator Bars—in 1994 and 1995 but eventually determined it wouldn't work when rolled out nationally.

Over the next five years, the energy bar market exploded, giving brand managers enough confidence to bring a Gatorade energy bar back in 2001.

Despite spending $28.2 million to advertise the energy bar in 2001 and 2002 (slogan: What Burns Inside You?), the bar had only 0.8 percent of the extremely crowded food/energy bar market by the end of its second year on shelves.[8]

"Line extension brands like Gatorade energy bars, Tanqueray Vodka, Smirnoff Black, Eveready Alkaline batteries, and Super Keds have gone nowhere," wrote Al and Laura Ries in their book *The Origin of Brands*. "What leads companies to make these classic marketing mistakes? It's a belief shared by many managers that marketing is a battle of brands. My brand versus your brand."[9]

There is often pressure on top brands to use their equity to quickly forge into different categories.

"We developed the energy bar for athlete performance, but we tried to market it too broadly," said Gatorade spokesman Andy Horrow. "We should have started it as a grassroots thing, but we went big. That's push and pull. You are worried about how you should market something at the same time you are worrying about the bottom line for Quaker or Pepsi."

Gatorade is a very powerful brand, and Pepsi is no doubt eager to help grow the profits it can make off its equity. The risk, as with any brand that means as much as Gatorade does, is that overextending the mark can devalue the core brand. By March 2005, Gatorade brand managers had once again given up on the energy bar idea, which became part of the brand's Performance Series.

Gatorade was able to grow its business by telling people exactly who it is and why you should drink it. Although there are plenty of occasions to drink Gatorade in a casual setting, under Quaker, Gatorade had tried not to advertise to that market. Brand managers had shown restraint in advertising to the mass public when they purchased the brand from Stokely.

Since Gatorade's early beginnings, doctors had used it in hospitals and recommended the sports drink to sick children who were dehydrated or were having problems with diarrhea. But Quaker officials wouldn't advertise to doctors because it would be straying from the core message and it was unclear whether doing so was legal under the FDA regulations.

A Gatorade competitor in the South, Suntory's 10-K, made a big marketing push in the mid-1990s to sell its product to doctors. Gatorade did reach pediatricians through a public relations and direct mail campaign to the medical community that talked about the merits of Gatorade. When it was pitched in this manner, the consumer who thought of Gatorade as the ultimate sports drink would never see the advertising.

"We also had to be careful that we didn't position the brand around an illness occasion," Sinopoli said. "How many times were you given something when you were sick and it stuck with you as the brand you associated with sickness?"

In the early 1990s, Gatorade's brand leaders lost focus, but they understood why what they were doing was wrong. For a short period of time, Gatorade's slogan was "Life Is a Sport. Drink It Up." This was clearly an attempt to open up, to advertise to those people who might drink the substance casually.

"We tried to be more inclusive," said one former Gatorade executive. "So the tagline was basically saying, 'If you participate in life, be part of our franchise.'"

The slogan was eventually buried, and the odds are that the future of Gatorade is filled with phrases that talk only to athletes. Those who happen to drink Gatorade while eating a pizza will be welcomed, but not in any overt way.

Throughout the history of the drink, the brand has been thought of as a special product. Part of this undoubtedly has to do with the fact that it is thought of as a bit strange. Perhaps David Whitford of *Fortune* magazine put it best when he said: "Gatorade looks like something Sam would serve with green eggs and ham. If you left some in a plastic cup at a doctor's office, they'd cap it and send it to the lab. Gatorade has three times more salt than Coke, half the sugar and none of the fizz."[10]

Over time, under Quaker and now Pepsi, that mystique—more formally described as "an aura of heightened value or interest or meaning surrounding a person or thing"—has stayed strong, thanks to the brand's staying on target the majority of the time.

Although the amount of incidental usage (people drinking Gatorade who are not working out) is increasing, Quaker officials discovered early on that the mystique will be broken if the brand is at all steered away from sports.

"The thing we learned is, never get away from your message," Marineau said. "You may have gardeners all over America slugging down Gatorade, but never show a guy mowing his lawn, never show a guy gardening."

In order for a product to be seen as unique, it has to be positioned in the right way. The Gatorade brand gets credit for being the originator of product placements in sports thanks to the coolers, the cups, and the towels, which still have a commanding presence in the athletic arena today. The less obvious part of the business that has made the Gatorade brand as strong as it is, is the relevance of its business plan.

Stokely-Van Camp's sports marketing strategy was never defined. The year before its acquisition by Quaker, Stokely's marketing staff devoted an enormous amount of time to its display at the World's Fair in Knoxville, Tennessee, since it was near the site of the company's beginnings. It might have looked good, but it didn't make much business sense.

Toward the end of Stokely's stint with Gatorade, most of the company's marketing dollars were being spent on being the primary sponsor of NASCAR drivers. This was also a personal buy: Stokely-Van Camp's headquarters was Indianapolis, and company chairman Bill Stokely loved the sport.

And while the number 88 "Big Bertha" Gatorade car had a strong run of drivers who won races in the late 1970s and early 1980s—the roster included Darrell Waltrip, Bobby Allison, Rusty Wallace, Ricky Rudd, and Geoff Bodine—having branding on a car in a sport that was primarily based in the Southeast wasn't exactly the best strategy for increasing the growth of Gatorade across the country. Once the marketers understood that there was more value in spending money on advertising that told people what the brand did for them than in plastering its logo on a car, Gatorade was on its way. It is about the sports imagery of Gatorade and ultimately getting to that Gatorade moment.

As brand managers for Gatorade continue to see their brand as a small piece of the pie in the active thirst market, straying away from the athletic occasion will be a temptation.

"The vulnerability to me is that you get so excited about that big opportunity and you somehow forget that you are a club, that you are for athletes, and that you won't ever do anything commercially that gets in the way of that," Wellington said. "And as you get bigger, if you are a marathoner, you start to say, if it's that big and it's available, how can it work for me?"

9. Form Smart Strategic Alliances

Gatorade had partnerships with trainers and athletes and many leagues, but its alliance with ESPN also helped the brand grow stronger. Over the years, investing in the network's programming through advertising has allowed the brand to be automatically prominent in the minds of sports fans, who are not only consumers but often active participants who fall into Gatorade's target market.

"We noticed ESPN in 1984," Marineau said. "We noticed that sports as entertainment was becoming absolutely huge, and it was going to be driven by all sorts of media choices that were out there."

So Gatorade tied itself to the rise of "The Worldwide Leader in Sports" as an early advertiser on the network. In 1995, when ESPN's web site, ESPNet SportsZone, was introduced, Gatorade was the very first advertiser. In 2003, when the web site—which had since been renamed ESPN.com—unveiled its new video capabilities in a product called ESPN Motion, Gatorade was, again, the very first advertiser.

In the summer of 2004, Gatorade continued one of the most powerful alliances in the sports world by putting out 1 billion of its bottles with the ESPN logo on them, commemorating the sports network's 25th anniversary. The alliance suggested by association that both were relevant in defining the sporting landscape for fans. Gatorade took this a step further by unveiling a limited edition "ESPN: The Flavor."

Large brands or companies that have relevant strategic alliances with many organizations are often pulled in different directions, since one company or brand is not kept in the loop with all the decisions made by the company or brand that it has a strategic alliance with.

In August 2003, ESPN launched an original football drama called *Playmakers*. Gatorade was featured through product placement in the shows and also advertised during commercial breaks. But throughout the show's two-and-a-half-month run, the NFL and the NFL Players Association were not happy with its portrayal of the behind-the-scenes lives of fictional football players, some of whom did drugs and were unfaithful to their wives. Concerned about its strategic alliance with the NFL, Gatorade elected to pull its advertising from the final show.

"We felt the show was in conflict with what we stand for as a brand," said Andy Horrow.[11]

Despite the show's solid ratings (averaging 1.6 million viewers for 11 episodes), ESPN executives also felt some pressure from their strategic alliance with the NFL and cancelled the show after its first season. (ESPN and its sister company ABC are owned by Disney and have the rights to *Sunday Night* and *Monday Night Football*.)

Part of having good strategic partnerships includes an equal give and take. When Marineau looked at the books on the royalty payments made to the doctors by Stokely-Van Camp, he said he discovered that the company had done almost everything it could to minimize the payments.

"We went in and said, 'Listen, we want to make this as transparent as possible,'" Marineau said. "We want to make sure that we have a very positive relationship with you, so let's make sure that we have a clear understanding of how this is calculated and that you are quite comfortable with it."

As part of the deal, Marineau asked the trust if it would be willing to invest in the business. A contract was worked out where in certain situations—introducing a new product, flavor, or package—the company would ask to take a year off from royalty payments on those products.

No good brand can continue to perform without making smart strategic alliances. In these partnerships, both sides have to be willing to share resources and trust each other, while always remembering that the individual brands come first in tenuous situations.

Gatorade is a unique brand whose brand managers are constantly researching the marketplace, learning from their mistakes, and seeking to reach the next consumer base through passion and emotion while striving to stay disciplined to its core message.

CHAPTER 9

Gatorade Critics

BY 1989, Dr. Robert Cade had received approximately $8 million in royalties from the sale of Gatorade. But he was working diligently to beat out the very product that he had helped invent and that had earned him a healthy fortune.

Along with his assistant, Malcolm Privette, and thermophysiologist Melvin Fregly, Cade was intent on making a better product. He felt that science had evolved, and he was confident that he could come up with a solution that would beat Gatorade in a head-to-head study. The new product would be called TQ2, shorthand for Thirst Quencher 2.

In May of 1989, he gave cyclists his new solution, and it beat out Gatorade in terms of pulse rate and change in blood volume. Cade said that TQ2 would give an athlete who drank the solution before exercise a 60 percent longer workout than water and a 30 percent longer workout than Gatorade.[1]

Cade accomplished this by adding the ingredients glycerol and pyruvate.

"Although Gatorade does help to combat some of the negative effects resulting from physical exertion, long distance runners and other athletes who must endure long periods of strenuous exercise still suffer the effects of decreased blood volume and a loss of energy-providing carbohydrates," reads the patent application. "The invention described here is a novel fluid composition which surprisingly and advantageously maintains blood volume at levels well above those observed in the absence of fluids or even with Gatorade. The novel product has the additional advantage of providing an energy source. Further, users of the product report lower levels of perceived difficulty of exercise when the novel fluid composition is used."[2]

Knowing that the University of Florida would probably want the new product, Cade agreed to assign the patent rights to the formula to the university. A company called Phoenix Advanced Technologies would license the product from the university for a starting fee of $25,000, and would produce it. Cade would become a paid spokesman for TQ2.

When Phoenix announced that the product would soon be unveiled, Cade told reporters that not only would it perform better than Gatorade, but it also tasted better than Gatorade. He acknowledged that he wasn't sure if it could ever surpass Gatorade's sales because "it's harder to launch an improvement than it is to start an original."[3]

Quaker and the Gatorade Trust were obviously not happy because they alleged that any sports drink improvements developed by Cade belonged to the trust, and through the trust to Quaker. So they sued Cade, Phoenix, and the University of Florida. Meanwhile, Phoenix continued to pitch its product to the beverage companies, including Pepsi.

Quaker Buys TQ2

Legal proceedings continued for two years, until Phoenix and Cade decided to settle. The two were embroiled in another lawsuit at the time over Cade's invention of Go!, a high-protein recovery drink for athletes. In July 1993, Phoenix sold TQ2 to Quaker Oats.

Quaker's purchase of TQ2 is certainly intriguing, especially given that the Gatorade formula that Quaker acquired from Stokely and Pepsi acquired from Quaker has remained relatively unchanged. When Stokely-Van Camp purchased the Gatorade concept from the doctors in 1967, the sugar, salt, and water solution didn't taste good enough to make it a commercial beverage, so Stokely scientists changed the palatability by adding sugar. Since then, ingredients have been added or replaced only because a newer ingredient that might have been safer or cheaper or provided a better taste profile became available. For example, preservatives like stannous chloride and sodium benzoate are no longer used, and soybean or vegetable oil (depending on the flavor) is in.

This lack of change has caused some people to be skeptical as to the true function of the Gatorade Sports Science Institute (GSSI), which has funded more than 120 studies over the past 17 years. Is GSSI there to develop the latest and greatest sports drink formula for the masses, or is it there to use science to best defend the status quo? Is it really possible that nothing substantial has come along in sports drink science over the last four decades that would make

Gatorade a better drink? There are, after all, very few product categories that fail to evolve over four decades.

Unlike Coca-Cola, whose formula—called "Merchandise 7X"—is so much of a secret that the company pulled the drink out of India after the government requested that the formula be made public, there is very little that is unique about Gatorade. And if one is to believe Dr. Louis A. Murray, who said in 1968 that Gatorade was just "a variation of the saline solution every hospital has been using for 10 years or more for heat prostration cases," the basic formula is almost a half-century old.

Dr. Bob Murray, now director of GSSI, has been working on the science of Gatorade since 1985. Murray insists that, as of the end of 2004, there are no ingredients that should be in everyday Gatorade that aren't there. Despite the fact that Quaker now holds the patent rights to TQ2, the company has never marketed the product. Murray says that TQ2 might have been touted as a better Gatorade, but GSSI, as well as outside research, concluded that Cade's key ingredients of glycerol and pyruvate didn't enhance the performance of a sports drink.

Cade, to this day, still stands by TQ2, saying that publication of the research behind the drink was stifled by Quaker.

GSSI's role, Murray stresses, is not a reactive, but a progressive one.

"The commitment from the company was and continues to be marvelous because right from Day 1 they said, 'Listen, we hired you because of your expertise. Go do the work that you need to get done, we'll support you doing so, and share the results with us and we'll make our business decisions accordingly,'" Murray said. "There's no real pressure to keep it the same way. In fact, if there is any pressure, it's to do whatever we can to try to make Gatorade more effective than it already is."

GSSI was created at a time when there was a lot of scientific controversy, since there wasn't much public evidence that Gatorade actually worked. Quaker wanted to make sure that it had a good product and that it could prove it. The company could do it with Gatorade in study after study. But it is undeniable that GSSI was also created to be part of Gatorade's powerful marketing arm. It was the defense mechanism enabling Quaker to develop the latest and greatest sports drink if need be, so that no one could make a sports drink that was better than Gatorade.

Luckily for the Gatorade brand, many of its potential competitors have made scientific claims, but didn't devote the time, energy, and capital to be able to counter GSSI when their various ingredients were questioned by studies, some commissioned by the sports drink giant.

Spending money on studies wasn't a priority for companies that were interested in building a beverage business. But it soon became apparent that, with Gatorade in the game, having some scientific research to say why a competing product was better was the barrier to entry in the sports drink industry. It was a barrier that many upstarts simply couldn't afford to overcome.

Pepsi's entry, All Sport, was easy for GSSI to shoot down. Formulating a sports drink with bubbles in it was idiotic. GSSI simply commissioned a study by Michigan State researchers. Magnetic resonance imaging (MRI) scans taken of subjects who ingested All Sport showed that their stomachs expanded so much that they pushed internal organs aside. No matter what its distribution system was, All Sport didn't have a chance.

With POWERade, Coca-Cola did invest in scientific research. GSSI still had something to say about POWERade's formula. It was a sweeter-tasting drink, a solution made with 2 percent more sugar than Gatorade. GSSI studies found that POWERade's 8 percent carbohydrate solution slowed the absorption of the drink by the body. Because the drink did not move into the small intestine—where most of the drink is absorbed—fast enough, more stomach upsets occurred with POWERade than with Gatorade, GSSI reported. Coca-Cola denied that there was a physiological difference.

From a public relations standpoint, the mere existence of GSSI says something to the consumer. Gatorade has developed a completely separate GSSI Web site, filled with everything any average consumer would want to know about the science of sweat.

"Gatorade promotes its laboratory and its institute," said Dr. Chris Carr, sports psychologist for the Methodist Sports Medicine Center in Indianapolis, Indiana. "When people see that the company has a lab, there's definitely a comfort level there that there isn't with Pepsi or Coke, companies that might be just making a diluted soft drink."

Pedialyte and Rehydralyte Challenge

Despite its goal of trying to be on the cutting age of sports drink research, Gatorade actually has been beaten to the punch.

While Gatorade did launch a pre-workout energy drink and a post-workout recovery drink as part of its Performance Series geared to professional and endurance athletes, it took 39 years to roll out a during-exercise drink for that market. This was perhaps out of fear that a new during-exercise product would suggest to the general public that there was a better Gatorade available, in much the same way that Gatorade Light suggested that there was a less-caloric Gatorade that could also do the job.

Since the early 1990s, GSSI had actually been considering the possibility of unveiling a during-exercise drink with more electrolytes.

But it wasn't until 2004 that Gatorade unveiled its Endurance Formula in powder form. Gatorade's brand managers almost had to do it if they wanted to own the sports drink market at every level. That's because specialty brands that appealed to this niche audience were becoming prevalent at endurance races and in professional locker rooms.

Ironically, two of the brands that were commonly being used by athletes didn't even target this audience. The athletes were drinking Rehydralyte and Pedialyte, solutions used to nourish children who were experiencing severe diarrhea. Rehydralyte and Pedialyte came in ready-to-drink 8-ounce bottles, and both were made by the same company, Abbott Laboratories, a company whose main headquarters is 48 miles away from the GSSI laboratory.

The appeal of these drinks was that they had more sodium. Larger football players were experiencing cramps, and Gatorade wasn't doing the trick. Even Dr. Randy Eichner, a professor of medicine at the University of Oklahoma who was on the GSSI Sports Medicine Review Board, admitted that the cramp-prone players on the Sooners football team were using Rehydralyte.[4]

The word started getting out that both Pedialyte and Rehydralyte were being used by Gatorade-sponsored teams.

Players at Ohio State and Tennessee supplemented their Gatorade use with Pedialyte on extra-hot days. Players on the Kansas City Chiefs (the very team that became part of Gatorade lore under the tutelage of Hank Stram) were quietly using Pedialyte.

In the fall of 1999, players on the highly ranked Penn State Nittany Lions football team—a school that was not sponsored by Gatorade at the time—sang Pedialyte's praises. For the first three games of the season, some players were cramping up, so they switched to the little bottles of Pedialyte.

"We have been conditioning all summer and we played in a few hot games already," said one of Penn State's star linebackers, Brandon Short. "But we need to just drink Pedialyte to stay hydrated and just be as smart as we can about rest."[5]

While Rehydralyte and Pedialyte were not marketing to the teams, it was a blow to Gatorade when players mentioned that they needed to use something other than Gatorade on extra-hot days. Gatorade had been making Gator Lytes, pills with sodium that were at least as effective as the sodium levels in Pedialyte and Rehydralyte, but it didn't have a drink. The Endurance Formula, which has almost twice the sodium and three times more potassium of regular Gatorade, now allows Gatorade to truly own the sidelines.

If nothing else, that situation proved that even though it has GSSI, Gatorade could be vulnerable to an attack from a research-based sports drink competitor. That competitor probably would never be able to make much of a dent in the mass market because of Gatorade's marketing power. But Rehydralyte and Pedialyte didn't even go after Gatorade. The fact that athletes were using something else that they deemed more effective than Gatorade forced Gatorade to make a move.

In fact, in 2005, Gatorade officials decided that there were enough athletes doing football two-a-days, playing all-day soccer tournaments, competing in three-hour bike races, and running marathons that it would be in the company's best interests to make the Endurance Formula available in ready-to-drink bottles on supermarket shelves. The product has a different look than standard Gatorade and comes in an odd 34-ounce size to further differentiate it.

Gatorade president Chuck Maniscalco called this launch "the most important product introduction ever in the Gatorade business."

"We believe we've got the proposition nailed," Maniscalco said. "We didn't want to put anything into the market until we had all the information on how it worked and how it could be best optimized.... We believe that if we have a better formula, as the pioneer in hydration efficiency, that it is positively unacceptable that any competitor unveils a product like this before we do."

But is it possible that Gatorade could get beaten to the punch again?

New Challenger

PacificHealth Laboratories is trying to make a run at it. The company, based in New Jersey, is headed by Dr. Robert Portman, a biochemist who was a former research scientist at Schering-Plough before starting his own pharmaceutical advertising firm, which proceeded his co-founding of the PacificHealth business.

In 2001, PacificHealth Labs developed a drink called Accelerade, which, like Gatorade, is meant to be used during exercise. The product claims to increase endurance by 24 percent over drinks of the same carbohydrate makeup. What made Accelerade different was that it was the first during-exercise drink to have protein in it.

Protein has always been thought to be essential for muscle repair. PacificHealth's recovery drink, Endurox R4, has protein in it, as does Gatorade's nutrition drink, which is meant to be consumed before or after exercise.

But up until Accelerade's debut, protein during exercise was thought to be a no-no, since it would slow the movement of the fluid through the body. Accelerade has a patent-pending four-carbohydrates-to-one-protein ratio that Portman says doesn't affect the digestion of the product when compared to other sports drinks.

"Gatorade always won the battles because they basically said they had the science behind them," Portman said. "And that was the key part. What we have now said to them is, 'Your science is old; our science is better, and we can prove it in study after study after study.'"

Portman is not trying to compete against Gatorade in stores. He knows that that is an impossible task. In 2004, his company was a $10 million brand. But he might be able to push Gatorade the way Rehydralyte and Pedialyte inadvertently did.

While Portman believes that other makers of sports drinks will add protein to their drinks over the next decade, he does not believe that Gatorade will ultimately adopt it. His reasoning? Making a change in the age-old Gatorade formula would not only cost money but increase the calories and make it more difficult for the drink to taste the same. The latter is especially a problem, he reasons, because he believes most people today drink Gatorade as an alternative to a soft drink instead of as a beverage to use before, during, or after working out.

Murray says that GSSI is still evaluating the merits of protein.

"Protein is something that we're keeping a close eye on," he said. "We've always believed that protein has a very important role in the recovery process, and we're continuing to look at it in that area. We remain unconvinced that protein during exercise provides any benefit—there's evidence on both sides of the fence regarding benefit during exercise, and we want to continue to work to make absolutely sure one way or the other whether protein has a role in a sports drink."

Gatorade vs. Water

Despite having resources that no other company that makes a sports drink has, Gatorade has steered away from going head-to-head with any particular drink in its advertising. It has, however, juxtaposed Gatorade with water, which executives see as their toughest competition for a piece of the active thirst market. Those with a critical eye can even raise objections to these advertisements.

Gatorade ran one ad in 1990 in many publications, including *Rolling Stone*, that was curiously vague in terms of presenting actual science to its consumers.

"We test Gatorade in laboratories. We test it at major universities, with sports science experts, on sophisticated scientific equipment with names that are longer than this sentence. What does it prove? Gatorade works."

The ad, with the headline "It works in theory. It works in practice," pointed the reader to a graph on the side comparing Gatorade to water. The graph showed that Gatorade helps provide a mean power output to the athlete of 200 watts, compared to 175 watts for an athlete drinking water. Missing is the label on one of the graph's axes that would tell the reader of the ad exactly how long one would have to exercise in order to receive this 25-watt advantage.

The answer is probably more than an hour of exercise, as there's little evidence that sports drinks can actually help improve performance if an athlete is exercising for less than an hour, unless the exercise is very vigorous.

"Sports drinks are useful in long races where you've dipped deeply into your energy reserves, but for any race that takes less than an hour, you'll never get depleted enough for them to have much effect," said Alberto Salazar, who won three straight New York City Marathons (1980 to 1982).[6]

Six-time Ironman champion Dave Scott says that drinks don't make a difference until someone has been racing for half a day or more.

"Though you do lose trace amounts of minerals during exercise, the degree to which electrolyte drinks are helpful in races under 12 to 15 hours is debatable," Scott wrote in his book *Dave Scott's Triathlon Training*.[7] Incidentally, Scott is now an endorser of Accelerade.

Another advertisement in which Gatorade pits itself against water ran on television in 2004. The ad was based on a study conducted by Dr. Mark Davis, professor and director of the Exercise Biochemistry Lab at the University of South Carolina, who is also on GSSI's Sports Medicine Review Board. The study showed that athletes playing in simulated games performed slightly better when they drank Gatorade instead of water.

While the study is technically fair and accurate, the comparison might be made more relevant by making the water a 6 percent sugar solution like Gatorade and then doing the head-to-head comparison.

That's what was done in 1990, at the University of Florida of all places. An exercise physiologist named David Criswell divided a high school team into two groups. The players simulated a football game. Half the athletes drank artificially sweetened colored water and half drank "a brand name sports drink," and Criswell saw no difference in performance.

"Football teams usually invest in these beverages because they expect them to make their players better athletes," Criswell said. "We wondered if it was true."[8]

GSSI's Murray says that Criswell's study was just one of many. A large number of studies, Murray says, have found that there are performance benefits from Gatorade over water.

To their credit, Gatorade officials have made a conscious effort not to overstate Gatorade's benefits. From the very beginning, the soft drink business was notorious for doing that. At the turn of the century, Coca-Cola was advertised as relieving mental and physical exhaustion, and Pepsi got its name from what it promised to do: cure dyspepsia, or upset stomach.

The Gatorade brand was only briefly in trouble for saying it did something that it did not. In the early days, Stokely officials had gone to the scientists to ask them how much faster than water Gatorade was absorbed by the body. One of them said that they were comfortable that Gatorade moved 12 times faster than water. So Stokely used the line vigorously in its advertising for at least the first two years.

That advertising was toned down somewhat in 1970, after Dr. Robert J. Murphy, the team doctor for the Ohio State Buckeyes, told a group of doctors at an American Medical Association meeting that Gatorade did not, in fact, travel through the body and get absorbed faster than water. Murphy was upset about the way the Stokely ads seemed to suggest that water was inferior.

"The thing that bothers me is [the idea] that water is 'no good,'" said Murphy, who said his teams would use only water to replenish on the field.

At the time, Dr. Cade responded to Murphy's claims as one might expect him to. "He's stupid and knows nothing of physiology, exercise or the body, or he didn't go to medical school," Cade said.[9]

But like Murphy, Quaker researchers eventually determined that, on average, the solution goes through the body and is absorbed as fast as water—still considered an accomplishment because the solution is not slowed by the carbohydrates.[10]

Influence Over Trainers

Critics have also questioned the connections that Gatorade has made in the business, a situation that has come along with its goal of being the most knowledgeable in exercise science. GSSI has more than 30 doctors on its Board of Advisors for Science and Education, its Sports Medicine Review Board, and its Nutrition Advisory Board.

GSSI does about one-third of its research in-house, while the rest is done at colleges and universities throughout the world. Gatorade officials maintain that there's nothing corrupt about either the commissioning of the work or the work itself.

"They [the scientists] would never put their names on the line," said Tom Fox, Gatorade's senior vice president of sports marketing. "Are you kidding? A scientist? Their reputation is gold. That's why GSSI has worked so well. It's not a physical location where we conduct our own research to prove what we want to prove—although we do conduct a great amount of research, and it's as good as anything else that's out there—but to be above reproach, we work with people around the world."

"I'm not saying that you couldn't find a doctor out there who would say that the 'Abcizer' is the greatest invention in the world for money," Fox said. "I would tell you that we find it offensive that anybody would ever imply that we would go out and try to get people to say something about what our product does to help athletes perform better that isn't absolutely true and supported by science."

Gatorade has been the highest-level sponsor of the American College of Sports Medicine since 1991 and enjoys official relationships with almost every major trainers organization. The Gatorade Company is the publisher of the semiannual newsletter of the Professional Football Athletic Trainers Society (PFATS), which includes a column on sports science by a GSSI member in each issue. Portman says that he believes Gatorade's relationship with trainers ultimately hurts the athletes.

"They influence trainers so much," Portman said. "They might not be on their payroll, but they've treated them so beautifully that the relationship comes to the detriment of the athlete, which is the real travesty behind all of Gatorade's marketing."

Despite Gatorade's many sponsorship deals, Fox says he won't do a deal with an organization if it does not intend to actually drink Gatorade.

"The only rule, and it's an unwritten rule, is that whatever the athletic trainer thinks he needs to fulfill the needs of his athlete, that's what he needs to do," Fox said. "If there was a better product out there, and the athletic trainer believed that that product was going to have a physiological benefit and it was proven, then I would encourage that athletic trainer to use the best product. The fact of the matter is, that's why we are going to be the best product."

In 1988, the Ohio State Buckeyes were no longer using water on the sidelines. Instead, they were using Exceed, a product made by Ross, a division of Abbott Laboratories, which also makes Rehydralyte. Ross was based in the Buckeyes' hometown of Columbus, Ohio.

Fox said that he wouldn't pay Ohio State for the sponsorship unless the university agreed that Gatorade was better. He provided materials from GSSI and contact information for Dr. Bob Murray, himself an Ohio State alum. After a couple of years, the school eventually agreed to switch.

"We have never, ever done a sponsorship that said, 'I know you don't believe in us, I know you don't think that we have the best product, but I'm going to pay you to use ours,'" Fox said. "That's not what we're all about."

Other scientists who have developed sports drinks say that they simply don't get a chance to make their drink the next Gatorade because of the sponsorships the brand controls.

Among those affected is University of New Mexico exercise physiologist Robert Robergs, inventor of Hydrade (motto: "The World's Fastest Sports Drink"). While the University of New Mexico's teams are technically free to drink Hydrade, they can't drink it from Hydrade containers. The institution has a reported eight-year, $1 million contract with Pepsi, Gatorade's keeper.

"What's meant to be a free market is locked in an arrangement with the University," Robergs said.[11]

Having the Gatorade Sports Science Institute does mean walking a fine line between educating the public on hydration and perhaps using GSSI to sell product.

Gatorade brand managers will tell you that educating the public is the number-one goal, but it's impossible to ignore the fact that GSSI is part of Gatorade, which is part of Pepsi, which is a public company that is expected to make money.

Current and past Gatorade employees say that the brand does more goodwill than most. Nearly every summer, an athlete dies from heatstroke. Gatorade officials could have used this to launch public campaigns about proper hydration. Instead, Gatorade has stayed away from doing that, while not staying away from the situation. Gatorade has typically sent information and product to the player's school district or to that state's coaches association, informing them how to avoid heatstroke and extreme dehydration.

"It was not to sell Gatorade," said P. J. Sinopoli. "We never told anyone we were doing it, and it was all free product. It was more of a corporate citizenry thing because we knew that the kid didn't have to die. If we turned those things into commercials or sent out press releases to tell everyone what we did, it would be wrong."

The Dehydration Myth

But there are those who say that GSSI overpromotes hydration in order to promote its product. South African exercise physiologist Timothy Noakes refers to this as the "dehydration myth."

Noakes argues that modest levels of dehydration in athletes are not of great consequence, as opposed to high levels of hydration, which could cause hyponatremia, in which people running long-distance races essentially dilute the sodium levels in their body so drastically that they could die. Noakes first wrote about the condition in 1985.

In July 2003, Noakes published an article in the *British Medical Journal* that got attention at Gatorade headquarters in Chicago.

"Exercisers must be warned that the overconsumption of fluid (either water or sports drinks) before, during or after exercise is unnecessary and can have a potentially fatal outcome," Noakes wrote. "Perhaps the best advice is that drinking according to the personal dictates of thirst seems to be safe and effective."[12]

Despite Noakes' hard stance in a well respected journal, hyponatremia didn't become a common term among long-distance runners in the United States until almost two years later. In April 2005, days before the running of the Boston Marathon, the *New England Journal of Medicine* reported that a substantial fraction of marathon runners (13 percent) tested at the 2002 Boston Marathon experienced some level of hyponatremia.

Although Gatorade wasn't mentioned in the report, it's easy to see how the brand would be targeted. Critics point to recommendations made by the Gatorade-affiliated National Athletic Trainers Association (NATA), which Gatorade includes in their literature. In general, the organization recommends drinking as much as 30 ounces of fluid before working out, seven to 10 ounces every 15 minutes, and at least 20 ounces per pound lost within two hours.

While Noakes could argue that this is overdrinking, Gatorade officials reason that harmful overdrinking rarely occurs compared to dehydration, which is more of an issue for the common athlete.

The salt in Gatorade actually promotes drinking, meaning that the term "thirst quencher" is actually a misnomer, since quenching thirst is never the ultimate goal.

"We know that, at the very least, Gatorade will encourage people to drink more," Murray said.

Those affiliated with GSSI also mention that in its report, the *New England Journal of Medicine* only briefly mentioned drinking sports drinks versus water. Drinking large amounts of Gatorade is better than water in this case, since hyponatremia occurs as a result of the dilution of sodium, which Gatorade (made up of 94 percent water) helps replenish.

Gatorade has used GSSI so effectively that Murray and the members of its board are often quoted in articles and seen on television to advise parents and young athletes about hydration in general. While GSSI and Gatorade are partly making a contribution to society in doing this, the institute is inextricable from business. This could lead to mixed messages.

Such a situation might exist in Gatorade's partnership with the University of North Carolina–Chapel Hill to cut down on childhood obesity.

Gatorade's Andy Horrow admits that the brand's $4 million campaign is not only good for brand equity but good for the brand "because if kids aren't active, they are less likely to be drinking Gatorade."

But if kids are active, does Gatorade in any way hurt a child's chances of using activity to lose weight in order to achieve the goal of being 100 percent hydrated at all times?

According to "Defeat the Heat," a public safety campaign that began in 2003 and was run by GSSI in coordination with the National Athletic Trainers' Association, a 100-pound child playing a sport for three hours should drink a minimum of 44 ounces of solution in order to be completely hydrated. If that drink is Gatorade, the intake is 330 calories.

While the program does not push Gatorade, its Web site does feature a graphic that points to the fact that children are likely to drink more if a sports drink is available, compared to water or flavored water.

"We need to realize how we compare something we eat or drink to the actual time it would take to burn off calories," said dietician Susan Kundrat. "Getting on a treadmill for 45 minutes may burn 300 calories, but you could drink 300 calories in two minutes."[13]

Gatorade officials say that their drink needs to include the calories it does in order to work effectively. In their defense, an 8-ounce serving of Gatorade has fewer calories (50) than beverages that have traditionally been labeled as healthy—orange juice (110 calories), apple juice (117 calories), and low-fat milk (121 calories).[14] In one of GSSI's pamphlets, entitled *Sports Drinks: Myths and Facts*, it is stated that research shows that consuming a sports drink during exercise, instead of water, will probably lead to an athlete's consuming fewer calories during the day.

No matter what the critics say or do, Gatorade seems to be nearly unassailable. Its storied history, its intricate marketing plan, its innovative sales team, and its scientific institute have all contributed in a very complex way to making it one of the strongest brands.

"We are pushing boundaries where we didn't go before," Maniscalco said. "You have to believe that some day there's going to be a wall and we're going to run into it, because this Gatorade product has defied gravity in this business."

Can Gatorade ever be out-Gatoraded? Perhaps in the scientific world. But if that happened, would that drink ever emerge from the niche market? If an ingredient proved to be scientifically viable, wouldn't Gatorade, at the very least, introduce it to hard-core athletes through its branded Performance Series line?

Do people really want the best drink to rehydrate themselves? Or do they want the best alternative to a soft drink to make their pizza go down more easily?

The future holds the answers. As for the past—who would have thought, when those four doctors were mixing the solution the night before its first test on the varsity team 40 years ago, that a drink that tasted like toilet bowl cleaner would have a story that was this sweet?

DR. ROBERT CADE still lives in Gainesville, Florida, and still has an office at the University of Florida. Despite having become a multi-millionaire, Cade still lives with his wife, Mary, in the same six-bedroom, three-bathroom home they have lived in since 1964. His other inventions include a novel shoe polish can, a hydraulic football helmet, Super Gator (a protein-enriched orange juice), and a patent on making a type of synthetic rubber. He collects Studebakers (he has almost 200 of them) and rare stringed instruments (14 violins, 2 violas, and 2 cellos). Said Cade: "I don't know that money makes happiness, but it sure makes life easier."[1]

Dr. Dana Shires lives in Tampa, Florida, in the house formerly owned by former Tampa Buccaneers quarterback Trent Dilfer. He and his family control 15 of the 101 shares in the Gatorade Trust.

Gatorade inventors, Dr. Jim Free, Dr. Alex DeQuesada, and Dr. Dana Shires, at a Gatorade Trust meeting in Tampa, Florida, February 17, 2005. (Matthew Troyer/Bingham McHale LLP)

Twenty years ago, Shires founded the LifeLink Foundation, a non-profit community service organization that has performed thousands of kidney, liver, pancreas, lung, and heart transplants.

Dr. Jim Free has retired from the daily practice of medicine. He serves on the LifeLink board and works as chairman of the Legacy Fund, established by LifeLink to increase public awareness of organ transplantation.

Dr. Alex DeQuesada arrived from Havana, Cuba, in 1960 with $5 in his pocket and the clothes he was wearing. Thanks to Gatorade royalties, DeQuesada is now retired and collects more than $5 a minute.

Claude Spilman, the attorney who negotiated the deal with Stokely on behalf of the Gatorade Trust, was put on dialysis in 1966—the same year he negotiated the contract. He received a new kidney in 1975 and died at the age of 62 in 1983, the year Stokely was bought by Quaker Oats.

Eugene Tubbs, one of the original financiers of Gatorade, was a physician in Rockledge, Florida, at the time of the Gatorade suit against the University of Florida. He later went to law school, passed the bar, and practiced law. In July 1978, Tubbs was caught in a thunderstorm in his single-engine plane. He and his wife, Carol, both died in the accident. Members of his family still hold shares in the trust.

Dr. John Donohue purchased two shares of Gatorade stock in the late 1960s for $55,000. In 1974, Donohue, a urologist, helped develop a chemotherapy and surgical regimen for testicular cancer that has saved thousands of lives. His best-known patient was six-time Tour de France winner Lance Armstrong. Today, his shares yield him at least $500,000 annually. "It was a really aggressive thing to put most of my free cash at the time into this one thing," Donohue says. "I'm still in awe that it turned out as it did. But I'd rather be lucky than smart."

Kent Bradley, the man who brought Gatorade to Stokely-Van Camp in 1966, died nine years later. But not before he sold some of his shares to a college roommate, J. Roy Dee.

The Gatorade Trust Family. (Matthew Troyer/Bingham McHale LLP)

As secretary to J. Roy Dee, who owned an oil drilling business in Mount Carmel, Illinois, Wilma Bolden received the opportunity to buy 1/25 of a share of Gatorade in the late 1960s for $1,000. Today, her investment brings in $10,000 a year. Said Bolden: "We were loyal employees, and he wanted to give something to us."

In 1967, Barth Green was a student at Indiana University's medical school when he met Shires and Bradley, who were both teaching at the school. When given a chance to buy into the trust, he borrowed $5,000 and bought a fifth of a share. "Every time I walk into the store, I'm so proud of what it has become," he says. Today, Green is a world-renowned neurologist who heads up the neurological surgery department at the University of Miami.

APPENDIX A

Sponsorships

GATORADE ATHLETES

Ricky Carmichael

Vince Carter

Landon Donovan

Kevin Garnett

Mia Hamm

Chamique Holdsclaw

Derek Jeter

Jimmie Johnson

Michael Jordan

Matt Kenseth

Mike Lambert

Kristine Lilly

Peyton Manning

Mark Martin

Ryan Newman

Mark Prior

Kerri Walsh

Abby Wambach

Yao Ming

NCAA SCHOOLS

Air Force Academy

Army Athletics

Ball State University

Bowling Green State
  University

Clemson University

Colorado State University

Duke University

East Carolina University

Georgetown University

Grambling State University
Indiana University
Kansas State University
Marshall University
Marquette University
Miami of Ohio
Mississippi State University
North Carolina State
   University
Northwestern University
The Ohio State University
Oklahoma State University
Penn State University
Pepperdine University
Purdue University
Seton Hall University
St. John's University
Stanford University
Syracuse University
Temple University
Texas A&M University
Texas Christian University
Tulane University
University of Alabama
University of Arizona

University of Arkansas
University of California
   –Berkeley
UCLA
University of Cincinnati
University of Colorado
University of Florida
University of Illinois
University of Mississippi
University of Nebraska
UNLV
University of Notre Dame
University of North Carolina
University of Tennessee
University of Texas
University of Virginia
University of Washington
University of Wyoming
Vanderbilt University
Villanova University
Virginia Tech University
Wake Forest University
Washington State University
West Virginia University

NCAA CONFERENCES

Atlantic Coast Conference
Big East Conference
Big Ten Conference

Big XII Conference
Conference USA
Metro Atlantic Conference

Mid-American Conference

Mountain West Conference

Pac 10 Conference

Patriot League

Southeastern Conference

NBA TEAMS

Atlanta Hawks

Boston Celtics

Charlotte Bobcats

Chicago Bulls

Cleveland Cavaliers

Dallas Mavericks

Denver Nuggets

Detroit Pistons

Golden State Warriors

Houston Rockets

Indiana Pacers

Los Angeles Clippers

Los Angeles Lakers

Memphis Grizzlies

Miami Heat

Milwaukee Bucks

Minnesota Timberwolves

New Jersey Nets

New Orleans Hornets

New York Knicks

Orlando Magic

Philadelphia 76ers

Portland Trail Blazers

Sacramento Kings

San Antonio Spurs

Seattle SuperSonics

Toronto Raptors

Washington Wizards

WNBA TEAMS

Charlotte Sting

Connecticut Sun

Detroit Shock

Houston Comets

Indiana Fever

Los Angeles Sparks

Minnesota Lynx

New York Liberty

Phoenix Mercury

Sacramento Monarchs

San Antonio Silver Stars

Seattle Storm

Washington Mystics

ALL NFL TEAMS

MAJOR LEAGUE BASEBALL TEAMS

Anaheim Angels

Chicago Cubs

Chicago White Sox

Cleveland Indians

Florida Marlins

Kansas City Royals

Milwaukee Brewers

Minnesota Twins

Pittsburgh Pirates

Toronto Blue Jays

ALL AVP TEAMS

ALL MAJOR LEAGUE LACROSSE TEAMS

COLLEGE FOOTBALL BOWL GAMES

Champs Sports Bowl

FedEx Orange Bowl

Liberty Bowl

Music City Bowl

Nokia Sugar Bowl

Outback Bowl

Rose Bowl presented by Citi

Tangerine Bowl

Tostitos Fiesta Bowl

Toyota Gator Bowl

MAJOR LEAGUE SOCCER

U.S. Men's National Team

U.S. Women's National Team

Chicago Fire

Colorado Rapids

Columbus Crew

Dallas Burn

D.C. United

Kansas City Wizards

Los Angeles Galaxy

New England Revolution

N.Y./N.J. MetroStars

San Jose Earthquakes

OTHER SOCCER

AFC Lightning SC

Austin United Capitals

Baltimore Bays SC

Challenge SC

Chicago Fire Juniors

Chicago Magic

Colorado Girls Soccer
   Academy

Colorado Rush SC

Crossfire Premier

D'Feeters SC

Eclipse Select

FC DELCO

FC Greater Boston

Irvine Strikers

Javanon SC

KCFC Alliance

Lake Oswego SC

Michigan Wolves/Hawks

New Orleans Soccer Academy

Players Development Academy

Pleasanton Rage Girls SC

Rosa Colorado SC

St. Louis SC

San Diego Surf SC

Santa Rosa United SC

Sereno SC

Sockers FC

So. Cal United SC

Stammers FC

Virginia Rush SC

West Kendall Optimist Soccer

NASCAR DRIVERS AND TEAMS

Bill Davis Racing

Hendrick Motorsports

Jimmie Johnson

Matt Kenseth

Mark Martin

MBV

Morgan-McClure

Ryan Newman

Penske Racing

PPI

NASCAR TRACKS

California Speedway

Chicagoland Speedway

Darlington Raceway

Daytona International
Speedway

Homestead-Miami Speedway

Kansas Speedway

Martinsville Speedway

Michigan International
Speedway

Nazareth Speedway

Phoenix International
Raceway

Richmond International
Raceway

Talledega Superspeedway

Watkins Glen International
Speedway

Gatorade also sponsors the
Daytona Qualifying event,
called "Gatorade Duel at
Daytona."

RUNNING EVENTS

Big Sur International Marathon

Bolder Boulder

Boston Marathon

Chicago Triathlon

Gasparilla Road Race

HP Houston Marathon

ING New York City Marathon

Ironman Triathlon

LaSalle Bank Chicago
  Marathon

Los Angeles Marathon

SBLI Falmouth 12K

HIGH SCHOOL COACHES ASSOCIATIONS

Arizona

California

Colorado

Connecticut

District of Columbia

Florida

Georgia

Illinois

Indiana (football)

Iowa

Michigan (basketball)

Minnesota

Mississippi

Montana

Nebraska

New York

North Carolina

Oklahoma

Oregon

Pennsylvania

South Carolina

South Dakota

Texas

Tennessee

Virginia

Wyoming

STATE ACTIVITY ASSOCIATIONS

Arizona

Arkansas

California

Florida

Illinois

Kentucky

Louisiana

Minnesota

North Carolina

South Carolina

Tennessee   Virginia

Texas

Gatorade is present on 8,700 high school sidelines.

SPONSORING ORGANIZATION OF:

American College of Sports Medicine (ACSM)

American Football Coaches Association (AFCA)

American Sports Education Program (ASEP)

Collegiate Strength and Conditioning Coaches Association (CSCCA)

National Athletic Trainers' Association (NATA)

National Basketball Trainers Association (NBTA)

National Strength and Conditioning Association (NSCA)

Professional Baseball Athletic Trainers Society (PBATS)

Professional Football Athletic Trainers Society (PFATS)

Sports, Cardiovascular and Wellness Nutritionists (SCAN)

Women's Sports Foundation (WSF)

Origins Ad

After research revealed that not many consumers in Australia knew about Gatorade's origin, Gatorade's brand managers decided to tell them a short version of the story behind the drink's beginnings.

"We say stuff the other guys can't," said Danny Schuman, group creative director at Element 79 Partners, who has been working on the Gatorade business since 1991. "They don't have a story. The other guys thought up their product in boardrooms; Gatorade was developed on the playing field."

A modification of the ad, using the following script, was introduced in the United States in 2002. Renowned college football announcer Keith Jackson narrates:

Keith Jackson: The legend was born in 1965 in the storied swamp of Florida. And as befits a legend, it began with a searing question:

Chip Hinton (freshman football player in 1965): Coach asked why we didn't pee during a game.

Dr. Robert Cade and Dr. Dana Shires: The players weren't properly hydrated and their performance suffered.

Keith Jackson: But salvation was nearby. As the Gators marched through the season, they drank an electrolyte-carbohydrate beverage created by the University of Florida scientists. Naturally they called it Gatorade. In conditions that would make a salamander sweat, the Gators thrived.

Jack Hairston (newspaper reporter): We outscored our opponents by 158 points in the second half.

Donna Kay Berger (cheerleader): Go Gators!

Keith Jackson: In 1967, when the Gators sealed their first-ever Orange Bowl win on a 94-yard scamper, Gatorade had arrived. Through decades of championships, and in ways the creators could only have imagined, the proving has continued.

Dr. Bob Murray: We've been testing athletes for decades, making Gatorade the most researched sports drink in the world.

Keith Jackson: Born on the hardscrabble gridirons of Florida; tested and proven by generations of athletes in the noble pursuit of greatness. But as the games never end, so the legend continues.[1]

Everywhere Rap

On January 1, 2004, L.L. Cool J became the first music artist to appear in a Gatorade commercial. The lyrics pay tribute to all the places where Gatorade can be found.[2]

Sandlots

Half Pipes

Half Courts

Center Court

Center Field

Rec Centers

Rec Leagues

Major Leagues

And Labs

Super Bowl

Fog Bowl

Windstorms

Windmills

Sweat Chambers

And Labs

Turf

Grass

Mud

Sand

Schoolyard

Backyard

The Garden

The Swamp

The Vet

The Met

The Pit

The Park

The Lake

The Jake

The BOB

Deandome

Skydome

And Labs

Venice

Rucker

Old School

New School

Home

Gatorade.

Tested in labs, proven everywhere.

Gatorade Royalties

Under the agreement struck with the University of Florida in 1972 the university receives 20 percent of all royalty payments. Those payments must be used for research-related projects at the university. During the first 10 years, the money was used primarily for a Gatorade professorship and research fund and a marine lab, with some money earmarked for the School of Medicine and the university libraries. Money from Gatorade continues to be used for scholarships and grants.

July 1, 1973, through June 30, 1984: $3,154,536
July 1, 1984, through June 30, 1993: $21,799,534
July 1, 1993, through June 30, 2003: $62,839,409
Total collected by the university from 1973 through 2003: $87,793,479[3]

Gatorade Sales

U.S. Market Share Statistics

Year	All Sport	Gatorade	POWERade
1993	2.9	82.4	5.9
1994	7.6	73.8	10.5
1995	9.8	72.3	12.1
1996	10.2	72.0	12.9
1997	9.6	73.1	14.3
1998	8.2	73.9	16.2
1999	6.5	76.1	16.0
2000	4.5	79.3	15.3
2001	2.6*	79.9	17.0
2002	1.8	81.2	16.6
2003	1.1	80.9	17.3[4]
2004	0.9	80.4	18.1

*Monarch/Pepsi

Here is how Gatorade has sold in the United States over the past decade (in cases). A case represents 192 ounces[5]:

1993	82.4 million	—
1994	155.4 million	+88.6 percent
1995	170 million	+9.4 percent
1996	190 million	+11.8 percent
1997	220 million	+15.8 percent
1998	260 million	+18.2 percent
1999	296 million	+13.8 percent
2000	325 million	+9.8 percent
2001	345 million	+6.2 percent
2002	403 million	+16.8 percent
2003	474 million	+17.6 percent
2004	546 million	+15.2 percent

U.S. SPORTS BEVERAGE MARKET

Wholesale Dollars

Year	Market Size[6]	Year	Market Size[6]
1985	$217 million	**1995**	$1.24 billion
1986	$284 million	**1996**	$1.39 billion
1987	$359 million	**1997**	$1.48 billion
1988	$474 million	**1998**	$1.69 billion
1989	$568 million	**1999**	$1.86 billion
1990	$676 million	**2000**	$2 billion
1991	$735 million	**2001**	$2.18 billion
1992	$800 million	**2002**	$2.41 billion
1993	$875 million	**2003**	$2.69 billion
1994	$1 billion		

All-Time Flavor Roster

Lemon-Lime (1967)

Orange (1969)

Fruit Punch (1983)

Lemonade (1987)*

Citrus Cooler (1989)

Tropical Fruit (1991)*

Grape (1993)*

Ice Tea (1993)*

Cool Blue Raspberry (1995)*

Wild Apple (1995)*

Lemon Ice (1995)*

Watermelon (1995)*

Cherry Rush (1996)*

Strawberry Kiwi (1996)

¡Mandarina! (1996)*

Glacier Freeze (1997)

Whitewater Splash (1997)*

Alpine Snow (1997)*

Riptide Rush (1998)

Midnight Thunder (1998)*

Fierce Lime (1999)*

Fierce Melon (1999)

Fierce Berry (2000)

Fierce Grape (2000)

High Tide (2001)*

Starfruit (2001)*

Passion Fruit (2001)*

Xtremo Mango Electrico (2002)

Xtremo Citrico Vibrante (2002)*

Xtremo Tropical Intenso (2002)

Ice Strawberry (2002)*

Ice Orange (2002)*

Ice Lime (2002)*

Cascade Crash (2002)

All-Stars Berry (2002)

All-Stars Strawberry (2002)

All-Stars Watermelon (2002)*

Fierce Strawberry (2003)

Ice Watermelon (2003)*

Berry Citrus (2003)

Cool Blue (Relaunched) (2003)

All-Stars Ice Punch (2004)

All-Stars Pink Lemonade (2004)

X-Factor Lemon-Lime + Strawberry (2004)

X-Factor Fruit Punch + Berry (2004)

X-Factor Orange + Tropical Fruit (2004)

ESPN The Flavor (2004)*

Lemonade (Relaunched) (2005)

Raspberry Lemonade (2005)

Strawberry Lemonade (2005)

Endurance Formula Fruit Punch (2005)

Endurance Formula Lemon-Lime (2005)

Endurance Formula Orange (2005)

All-Stars Tropical Punch (2005)

Cooler Orange (2005)

* Defunct

APPENDIX B

QUAKER

The Quaker Oats Company, Merchandise Mart Plaza, Chicago, Illinois 60654

January 7, 1987

Mr. William Parcells
Head Coach
New York Giants
Giants Stadium
East Rutherford, NJ 07073

Dear Coach Parcells:

We at The Quaker Oats Company, makers of **GATORADE®** Thirst
Quencher, realize that due to the year-long "**GATORADE**
dunking" you have been receiving your wardrobe has probably
taken a beating.

The enclosed should help remedy this problem; after all
we do feel somewhat responsible for your cleaning bill.

Wishing you the best of luck this weekend.

Sincerely yours,

William D. Schmidt
Director, Sports Marketing

WDS/dk
Enclosure

January 9, 1987

Mr. William D. Schmidt
Director, Sports Marketing
The Quaker Oats Company
Merchandise Mart Plaza
Chicago, IL 60654

Dear Mr. Schmidt:

I would like to sincerely thank you for the $1,000.00 gift certificate you sent me for Brooks Brothers. It's a very kind and generous gift, and I appreciate your thoughtfulness more than you can know.

It's quite hectic and busy around here at this point but we're continuing to work hard to hopefully win the next two.

Again, many many thanks for the gift certificate. It will be put to good use, and I certainly hope that I'll be getting a few more GATORADE dunkings this year.

My best wishes.

Sincerely yours,

Bill Parcells
Head Coach

BP:KK

NOTES

INTRODUCTION

1. Nielsen Monitor-Plus.

2. Fred Mitchell, "Durham's Glove Took Bath in Playoff Before Cubs Did," *Chicago Tribune*, Feb. 22, 1985, p. C1.

3. Philip Hersh, "Churning Away in Spitz' Image," *Chicago Tribune*, July 4, 2004, p. C1.

4. Anheuser Busch Annual Report, 2003.

5. John Crisafulli, *Backstage Pass: Catering to Music's Biggest Stars* (Nashville, Tenn.: Cumberland House Publishing, 1998).

6. Glenn Danforth, David Stirt, and Danny Wuerffel, *Florida: Saturdays at the Swamp* (Champaign, Ill.: Sports Publishing, 2004), p. 74.

7. "Gatorade Challenges Water Cooler," Associated Press, May 25, 2000.

8. Provided by Gatorade and *Beverage Digest.*

9. Gatorade, "How Well Do You Know Your Sports Drink?" press release.

CHAPTER 1

1. Bob Henderson, "Clearwater Doctor Sips Sports Drink of Success," *St. Petersburg Times*, Oct. 19, 1996, p. 1.

CHAPTER 2

1. Red Smith, "Florida Finds Its Stamina in Gatorade," *The Washington Post*, Sept. 10, 1967, p. B4.

2. Furman Bisher, "Dr. Cade's Magic Elixir," *Tampa Tribune-News*, May 31, 1970, pp. G1–G3.

3. Neil Amdur, "Florida's Pause That Refreshes: 'Nip of Gatorade,'" *Miami Herald*, Nov. 30, 1966, p. 4D.

4. "Doctor Puts Punch in Team Water," *The Washington Post*, Dec. 15, 1966, p. K1.

CHAPTER 3

1. Steve Snider, "Orange Juice, Gatorade Mix Well on Grid," United Press International, Nov. 18, 1967.

2. Ibid.

3. Gil Rogin, "The Bottle and the Babe," *Sports Illustrated*, July 1, 1968, p. 54.

4. Ibid., p. 57.

5. "Gatorade Brigade," *Newsweek*, Oct. 7, 1968, p. 90.

6. Elvis Presley, *Elvis: Live in Las Vegas*, BMG, 2001.

7. Howard Schmeck, Jr., "Government Officially Announces Cyclamate Sweeteners Will Be Taken Off the Market Early Next Year," *The New York Times*, Oct. 19, 1969, p. 58.

8. Terry Robards, "U.S. Curb on Sweeteners Triggers Frantic Trading," *The New York Times*, Oct. 21, 1969, p. 61.

9. Today, cyclamate is still banned in the United States, but it is used in products throughout the world. A decade later, saccharin was also found to cause cancer in animals, but Congress nixed the FDA's proposal to ban it. Products still contain saccharin today, but since 1977, they've had warning labels mentioning that studies show that it causes cancer in animals.

10. Origins 2: Behind the Scenes Footage, May 2003.

CHAPTER 4

1. Robert Cade, *Freut Euch des Lebens*, unpublished autobiography.

2. Scientific Research, Jan. 20, 1968.

3. Frank Murray, "Nationwide Scandal Brews on Gatorade Drink," *Tallahassee Democrat*, Oct. 25, 1968, p. 6.

4. "Gatorade 'Father' Suing U.S.," United Press International, Jan. 24, 1970.

5. Letter from Stephen O'Connell to Manuel Hiller, May 30, 1969.

6. "Dr. Cade Says His $2 Million Offer Not 'Ridiculously Low,'" *The Gainesville Sun*, May 18, 1969.

7. Peter H. Peugh, "Gatorade's Fast-Growing Popularity Stirs Royalty Fight Involving U.S., University," *The Wall Street Journal*, Dec. 18, 1969, p. 13.

8. Carol Brady, "Federal Government Files Suit to Gain Gatorade Rights," *The Independent Florida Alligator*, Aug. 12, 1971, p. 13.

9. "The Gator Fumble," editorial, *The Gainesville Sun*, Aug. 8, 1972.

CHAPTER 5

1. Aaron Kuriloff, "Showers Likely: Giants' Ritual of Dousing Winning Coach With Gatorade Won't Go Away," (New Orleans) *The Times-Picayune*, Jan. 27, 2001, p. 1.

2. Tony Kornheiser, "Parcells: One of the Guys," *The Washington Post*, Jan. 27, 1987, p. 1E.

3. Jim Burt and Hank Gola, *Hard Nose: The Story of the 1986 Giants*, (New York: Harcourt, 1987), p. 121.

4. Fred Lief, "Commentary," United Press International, Jan. 8, 1987.

5. "Most Memorable Super Bowl Moments," ESPN.com, p. 2.

6. Donnie Radcliffe, "The President's Spirited 76th," *The Washington Post*, Feb. 7, 1987, p. C3.

7. George Diaz, Alex Marvez, and Russ White, "Spurrier's Revenge," *Orlando Sentinel*, Nov. 11, 1990, p. C7.

8. "George Allen, Coach, Dead at 72; Led Redskins to Super Bowl VII," Associated Press, Dec. 31, 1990.

9. Ken Blanchard and Don Shula, *The Little Book of Coaching: Motivating People to Be Winners* (New York: Harper Business, 2001), p. 93.

10. Phil Arvia and Steve McMichael, *Steve McMichael's Tales From the Chicago Bears Sideline* (Champaign, IL: Sports Publishing, 2004), pp. 75–76.

11. Barry Rozner, "Hampton Robbed of Credit for Inventing 'Gatorade Dunk,'" (Chicago) *Daily Herald*, Nov. 25, 1999, p. 1.

CHAPTER 6

1. Sands, Taylor, Woods & Co v. Quaker Oats Co., "Proposed Findings of Fact and Conclusions of Law With Respect to Damages," U.S. District Court, Northern District of Illinois, June 21, 1993, pp. 8–9.

2. Ibid., p. 19.

3. Mary Beth Simmons, "Self Testing: Quest for Quenching Is Personal at Quaker," Tempo, *Chicago Tribune*, Jan. 10, 1993, p. 1.

4. Copyright © 1991 by Gatorade. Used with permission.

5. Jerry Bonkowski, "Gatorade Adds Jordan to Team," *USA Today*, Aug. 9, 1991, p. 2C.

6. Wicke Chambers and Spring Asher, "Getting Ahead Buyers' Question: 'What's in It for Me?' Personalized Messages Sell," *Atlanta Journal-Constitution*, June 22, 1992, p. B9.

7. Bob Garfield, "'Mike' Spikes Gatorade's New Jordan Advertising," *Advertising Age*, Aug. 12, 1991, p. 26.

8. Bob Greene, *Hang Time: Days and Dreams with Michael Jordan* (New York: St. Martin's Press, 1993), pp. 265–266.

9. "Should They Still 'Be Like Mike?'" *Advertising Age*, June 14, 1993.

10. Dan LeBatard, "Michael Jordan Shows Why He's the Best With

Timing of Latest Performance," *Miami Herald*, June 12, 1997.

11. Darrell Fry, "Bulls Battle Back," *Salt Lake Tribune*, June 12, 1997, p. 1C.

CHAPTER 7

1. Mark Pendergrast, *For God, Country & Coca-Cola: The Definitive History of the Great American Soft Drink and the Company That Makes It* (New York: Basic Books, 2000), p. 463.

2. Al Ries and Laura Ries, *The Origin of Brands: Discover the Natural Laws of Product Innovation and Business Survival* (New York: Harper Business, 2004), p. 140.

3. Ibid., p. 201.

4. Pendergrast, p. 98.

5. Jonathan Bond and Richard Kirschenbaum, *Under the Radar: Talking to Today's Cynical Consumer* (New York: Wiley, 1997), p. 63.

6. Rick Kash, *The New Law of Demand and Supply* (New York: Doubleday, 2002), p. 201.

7. Jim Aitchison, *How Asia Advertises: The Most Successful Campaigns in Asia-Pacific and the Marketing Strategies Behind Them* (New York: Doubleday, 2002), p. 201.

8. Beverage Digest research.

9. Dave Carpenter, "Science of Sweat Pays Off for Gatorade," Associated Press, May 23, 2000.

10. Data compiled by the National Association of Convenience Stores (NACS).

11. Research by Packaged Facts, calendar year 2003.

12. Diane Brady, Julie Forster, and Dean Foust, "Gotta Get That Gator," *BusinessWeek*, Nov. 27, 2000, p. 91.

13. Steve Matthews, "Coke Sees Growth in Sports Drinks: Targeting the Health Conscious," *Calgary Herald*, Apr. 25, 2004, p. E3.

14. Albert Chen, Frank DeFord, and Rick Lipsey, "Scorecard," *Sports Illustrated*, Oct. 8, 2001, p. 29.

15. Kenneth Hein, "Strategy Powerade Shakeup Exec Warns: Rival 'Gatorade's Going Down,'" *Brandweek*, May 21, 2001.

16. Darren Rovell, "POWERade FLAVA23 Hits Shelves Next Month," ESPN.com, Aug. 18, 2004.

17. Civil War Confederate Lieutenant General Nathan Bedford Forrest, not Napoleon, is most often credited with proclaiming this battle strategy.

CHAPTER 8

1. Rick Kash, *The New Law of Demand and Supply* (New York, Doubleday, 2002), p. 191.

2. "Is Stokely Worth Quaker's Lofty Bid?" *BusinessWeek*, Aug. 1, 1983.

3. Diane Brady, Julie Forster, and Dean Foust, "Gotta Get That Gator," *BusinessWeek*, Nov. 27, 2000, p. 91.

4. Stokely executives say that when they tested the product when they first acquired it, their tests showed that it did in fact move twelve times faster than water.

5. Joe Musser, *The Cereal Tycoon: Henry Parsons Crowell, Founder of the Quaker Oats Co.* (Chicago: Moody Publishers, 1997), p. 89.

6. Jim Kirk, "Quaker Brings Out Gatorade Light, Aid for That Deep Down Body Fat," *Adweek*, Apr. 16, 1990.

7. Paul Simao, "Drink Firms Bet on Flavoured Water," Reuters, Dec. 13, 2004.

8. *The U.S. Market for Food Bars: Cereal, Snack, Sports, Meal Replacement*, Packaged Facts, a publishing division of MarketResearch.com, September 2003.

9. Al Ries and Laura Ries, *The Origin of Brands: Discover the Natural Laws of Product Innovation and Business Survival* (New York: Harper Business, 2004), p. 288.

10. David Whitford, "The Gatorade Mystique: It's Salty. It's Fluorescent. It's Wildly Popular," *Fortune*, Nov. 23, 1998, p. 44.

11. Tom Lowry, "Gatorade Sacks ESPN's Playmakers," *BusinessWeek Online*, Nov. 7, 2003.

CHAPTER 9

1. Barbara Lloyd, "Gatorade Challenged," *The New York Times*, Dec. 24, 1990, p. 42.

2. Robert Cade, Melvin J. Fregly, and Malcolm Privette, "Compositions and Methods for Achieving Improved Physiological Response to Exercise," filed. Jan. 17, 1989, date of patent Jan. 1, 1991.

3. Denise L. Amos, "Battling the Gator for Market Share," *St. Petersburg Times*, Nov. 25, 1990, p. 1I.

4. Randy Eichner, "Sports Drinks Aid Salty Players," *Daily Oklahoman*, July 9, 1999, p. I2.

5. William Kalec, "Penn State Babying Themselves to Prepare for Miami Weather," *Daily Collegian*, Sept. 17, 1999.

6. Alberto Salazar, *Alberto Salazar's Guide to Running* (International Marine Publishing, 2002), p. 192.

7. Dave Scott, *Dave Scott's Triathlon Training* (New York: Fireside, 1986), p. 100.

8. Betty Cortina, "Study: Sports Drink Claims Fizzle on Field," *Gainesville Sun*, Mar. 21, 1990.

9. Patti Bridges, "OSU Doctor Clarifies Gatorade Statements," *Gainesville Sun*, July 24, 1970.

10. Since some Stokely employees insist that Gatorade tested out at 12 times faster than water, it is possible that new ingredients slowed the speed of the solution.

11. Rivkela Brodsky, "Gatorade Present Throughout U. of New Mexico Campus," *Daily Lobo*, Dec. 3, 2004.

12. Michael Woods, "Study: Fitness Buffs Should Not 'Stay Ahead' of Thirst," Scripps Howard News Service, July 18, 2003.

13. Judy Hevrejs, "Energy Drinks May Be Giving You More Than You Asked," *Chicago Tribune*, July 29, 2004.

14. From Pepsi and the USDA.

EPILOGUE

1. Corey Flowers, "Gatorade Inventors Share Story at U. Florida Leaders Seminar," *The Independent Florida Alligator*, Feb. 26, 2001.

APPENDIX

1. Copyright © by Gatorade/Element 79. Used with permission.

2. Copyright © by Gatorade/Element 79. Used with permission.

3. Provided by the University of Florida.

4. *Beverage Digest* research.

5. Statistics provided by *Beverage Digest*.

6. Statistics provided by Beverage Marketing Corporation.

INDEX

Allen, George, 88–89
Amdur, Neil, 33–34, 54
Anheuser Busch, 4
Ashe, Arthur, 55
Auburn Tigers, 29, 51–52, 134

Bayer Bess Vanderwarker 105
  Pitzel, Bernie 105–107, 108, 110
Baby Gators, 19, 29
Baylor, Elgin, 54
Board of Regents, 68, 71–73
Bradley, Kent, 38, 41–46, 67, 213
Bryant, Paul "Bear," 13
Burt, Jim, 78–79, 81, 90

Cade, Robert, Dr., 9-12, 15–18,
  20–23, 25–27, 30–38, 50,
  54–55, 58, 65–67, 69, 71–73,
  75, 136, 152, 191–194, 203,
  211
Carson, Harry, 78–80, 82, 84,
  90–91
Chicago Bulls, 3, 99, 112, 116–118

Circle of Champions, 170–171
Coca-Cola, 4, 31, 36, 46, 61, 64,
  123–150, 152, 162, 172, 176,
  178, 183–184, 186, 194–196,
  202
  distribution, 127, 130–131
  marketing, 99, 101–105,
    132–137
  New Coke, 176
  possible partnership with
    Quaker, 123–124
  POWERade (*see* POWERade)
  pricing wars, 129
  six-pack, 172
convenience store strategy, 139-
  142
Crowell, Henry Parsons, 156
cyclamate, 58–63

dehydration, 10-11, 13, 17, 26, 63,
  206–209
DeQuesada, Alex, Dr., 12, 15, 23,
  37, 67, 212

Disney
  Jungle Book, The 106, 110
Dodd, Bobby, 35, 91
Douglas, Dewayne, 9
Element 79, 136, 160, 179
ESPN, 113, 146, 188–189
  ESPN.com, 188
  ESPN: The Flavor, 189
  SportsCenter, 110

Falk, David, 101–104, 115
Food & Drug Administration,
  59, 61
flavors, 46-47, 226
Florida/Georgia Game
  The World's Largest Outdoor
    Cocktail Party, 30
Florida State Seminoles, 112, 134
Fox, Tom, 92–93, 109, 114, 148,
  157, 162, 165–167, 169,
  204–205
Free, Jim, Dr., 15, 23, 66, 212

Gatorade alternatives,
  10-K, 185
  Accelerade, 199, 201
  Bengal Punch, 64
  Bulldog Punch, 63
  Gookinaid, 52
  Hydrate, 205–206
  Olympade, 64, 125
  Pedialyte, 197–198, 200
  Powerburst, 6, 179
  Rehydralyte, 197–198, 200,
    205
  Sportade, 28, 52
  "Take 5," 36, 52

Thirst Quencher 2 (TQ2),
    191–194
  water, 200–203
Gator-Aid, 23
Gatorade Bath (*also* Dunk, Shower,
    Splash), 77–78, 80–84, 86–91
Gatorade Energy Bar, 184–185
Gatorade Frost, 177
Gatorade Light, 175-178, 196
Gatorade Sports Science Institute
    (GSSI), 6, 100, 145, 156–157,
    168, 193–197, 200, 202–209
Gatorade Trust, 45–46, 66, 69, 74
Gatorgum, 182–183
Georgia Bulldogs, 30–33, 63, 87
Georgia Tech, 35, 91
Graves, Ray, 12–15, 19–23, 26–27,
    31–33, 35, 37, 42, 56, 62, 70,
    136
Greene, "Mean" Joe, 133, 181

Hamm, Mia, 119–121
Hanover, Manfred, 4
Hispanic marketing, 171–172
  ¡Mandarina!, 171
  Xtremo, 171
hyponatremia, 206–208

James, LeBron, 148–150
Jordan, Michael, 2, 108–122,
    135–136, 173
  "23 vs. 39," 122
  Air Jordans, 111, 117
  baseball career, 116–117
  basketball comeback, 118–119
  "Be Like Mike," 2, 99–113,
    119, 122

Jordan, Michael (*cont.*)
  gambling, 115
  "Michael vs. Mia," 120
  retirement, 115–116
  second basketball comeback, 121

Kramer, Jerry, 51

Learned, Vincent, 26, 68
Long Beach State 49ers, 88–89
Louisiana State University, 15, 21,
  23, 87, 112
"Love Hurts" advertisement,
  180–181

Madden, John, 80, 91
Malawer, Sidney, 12, 17
Malgara, Giulio, 95–96, 99, 102
Maniscalco, Chuck, 160, 162, 165,
  179, 198
Marineau, Phil, 84, 97, 137, 142,
  147, 154, 156, 158, 163–164,
  173, 186, 188–190
McVay, Dave, 45
Midnight Thunder, 177–178
Monte Cristo No. 2 Cuban tor-
  pedo cigars, 114
Morriss, Guy, 86–87
Murray, Bob, 157, 194, 205

Namath, Joe, 15
NASA, 168
NASCAR, 83, 150–152, 187
  Gatorade In-Car Drinking
    System (G.I.D.S.), 150
  Gatorade vs. POWERade,
    150–152

New York Giants, 78–79, 81–84,
  89–91
Neyland, General Robert Reese,
  13
NFL, 2-3, 7, 50–51, 56, 78, 80,
  84–85, 135, 164–168, 170,
  178, 184, 189
Nike, 5, 99–101, 109, 111, 146,
  167, 176, 180
Notre Dame, 49

O'Connell, Stephen, 70, 73
Ohio State University, 197, 203,
  205
Olympic Games,
  1968, 52
  1972, 125
  1984, 125, 181
  1992, 134
  1996, 138–139, 180
  2002, 122
Oza, Rohan, 145, 152

packaging, 172-175
  12-ounce bottle, 175
  20-ounce bottle, 175
  EDGE, 174
  PET plastic bottles, 173
  plastic gallon bottle, 175
  squeezable sports bottle, 174
  wide-mouth bottles, 173
Parcells, Bill, 78–82, 84, 90–91
Pepsi, 4, 61, 126–135, 137-138
  141–145, 147, 152, 162, 172,
  178-179 183–184, 186,
  195–196, 206
  All Sport, 129, 132, 144, 195

Pepsi (*cont.*)
  distribution, 127, 130–131
  marketing, 99, 132–137
  Mountain Dew Sport, 126, 129,
    131–132
  Pepsi Challenge, 128
  pricing wars, 129
  purchasing Quaker, 144
  SoBe, 144
Performance Series, 157, 166, 196,
    209
  Endurance Formula, 166, 196,
    198
  energy bars, 185
  nutrition shakes, 166
Phelps, Michael, 4
Playboy Magazine, 56–57
POWERade, 6, 124, 126–128
    134–136, 138–139, 142–152
    174, 195–196
  FLAVA23, 149
  NASCAR battleground, 150–152
  relaunch, 145–150
  sponsorship, 104, 134, 138
  taste vs. effectiveness, 128–129
Presley, Elvis, 5, 57–58
Procter and Gamble
  Sunny Delight, 174
Propel, 145, 177, 183–184
Purdue Boilermakers, 49

Quaker, 6-7, 78, 81–84, 95–99,
    101, 103, 106, 108–109, 113,
    115, 119–120, 123–124, 135,
    139, 143–145, 153–156,
    158–160, 172–173, 176–178,
    181–187, 192–195, 203

Quarry, Jerry, 37

Reagan, Ronald, 82
Red Bull, 125
Rentz, Larry, 14, 19–20
Roddick, Andy, 146
Rogin, Gil, 53–54
Royal Crown, 56, 62

Sanders, Deion, 135
Schmidt, Bill, 80-82, 84–85, 91,
    95–96, 99, 101–105, 115–116,
    138, 163–166, 169–170, 178
Shires, Dana, Dr. 10–12, 15,
    17–18, 21, 27, 32, 35, 38,
    41–43, 46, 61, 67, 74,
    211–212
slogans,
  "Gatorade. Thirst Slayer," 181
  "Gatorade is thirst aid for that
    deep down body thirst!,"
    97–98
  "Is It in You?" 160, 180
  "Life Is a Sport, Drink It Up,"
    186
  "The Big Thirst Quencher," 56
  "What Burns Inside You?" 184
Smith, Larry, 19–20, 27
Smithburg, Bill, 115, 155
Southeastern Conference (SEC),
    10, 26–27, 30
Spilman, Claude, 44, 46, 61, 71,
    74, 212–213
Sports Illustrated, 4, 53, 116, 146
Spurrier, Steve, 27–29, 31, 35–36,
    87–88, 136
Stern, David, 135

Stokely, Alfred, 38, 45, 155
Stokely-Van Camp, 38, 41–58,
    61–67, 71–74, 78, 97, 153,
    163 181–182, 187, 189, 193,
    202, 212–213
Stokely, William Jr., 43
Stram, Hank, 62–63
Sullivan, George, 67
Sunbolt, 183
Super Bowls,
    IV, 63
    XXI, 82–83
    XXIII, 85
    XXXIX, 92
    XXXVII, 122
Suter, Emmanuel, 68
Sveda, Michael, 58, 60

TORQ, 166
trainers, 163-166, 204–205
Tubbs, Eugene, 36, 44–46, 72, 74,
    213

United States Olympic
    Committee, 122

University of Florida, 5, 7, 9–10,
    15, 25, 33–36, 38, 42, 51, 58,
    64–68, 70–72, 74–75, 87,
    192–193, 202, 213
University of Kentucky, 13, 38–39,
    86–87, 165
University of North Carolina-
    Chapel Hill, 119, 208
University of Tennessee, 13, 39,
    42, 197
UNLV Running Rebels, 83, 89

Verrett, Jacqueline, 59–60
Vick, Michael, 146

Wal-Mart, 117–118
Warren, Hank, 41–42, 44–45, 47,
    73
Washington Redskins, 19, 78, 81,
    88
Wellington, Sue, 117, 120, 162,
    166–167, 174, 177–178, 188
West, Jerry, 54

Zyman, Sergio, 125, 138, 143

ABOUT THE AUTHOR

Darren Rovell is the sports business reporter for ESPN.com. He appears on numerous ESPN radio affiliate shows, analyzes the sports business world for ESPNEWS, and contributes to ESPN's flagship *SportsCenter* and its investigative show *Outside the Lines.*

In 2004, Rovell was named to NewsBios' "30 Under 30," a list of the top 30 national business reporters under the age of 30.

Rovell is co-author of *On the Ball: What You Can Learn About Business from America's Sports Leaders,* which was published by Financial Times Prentice Hall. He graduated cum laude from Northwestern University in Evanston, Illinois.

Since 1988, he has consumed thousands of bottles of Gatorade. During his running of the 2004 New York Marathon, he drank 38 cups of it. He can be reached at TheGatoradeGuy@aol.com.